SECOND TO NO MAN BUT THE COMMANDER IN CHIEF

Hugh Mercer

AMERICAN PATRIOT

Michael Cecere

HERITAGE BOOKS
2015

HERITAGE BOOKS
AN IMPRINT OF HERITAGE BOOKS, INC.

Books, CDs, and more—Worldwide

For our listing of thousands of titles see our website
at
www.HeritageBooks.com

Published 2015 by
HERITAGE BOOKS, INC.
Publishing Division
5810 Ruatan Street
Berwyn Heights, Md. 20740

International Standard Book Numbers
Paperbound: 978-0-7884-5622-0
Clothbound: 978-0-7884-6122-4

Contents

About the Author

Michael Cecere Sr. teaches American history at Robert E. Lee High School in Fairfax County, Virginia, and was named the 2005 Outstanding Teacher of the Year by the Virginia Society of the Sons of the American Revolution. Mr. Cecere also teaches American history at Northern Virginia Community College. An avid Revolutionary War re-enactor, he currently is the commander of the 7th Virginia Regiment and participates in numerous living history events throughout the country. This is his eleventh book.

Other books by Michael Cecere

They Behaved Like Soldiers: Captain John Chilton and the Third Virginia Regiment, 1776-1778 **(2004)**

An Officer of Very Extraordinary Merit: Charles Porterfield and the American War for Independence, 1775-1780 **(2004)**

Captain Thomas Posey and the 7th Virginia Regiment **(2005)**

They Are Indeed a Very Useful Corps: American Riflemen in the Revolutionary War **(2006)**

In This Time of Extreme Danger: Northern Virginia in the American Revolution **(2006)**

Great Things Are Expected from the Virginians: Virginia in the American Revolution **(2008)**

To Hazard Our Own Security: Maine's Role in the American Revolution **(2010)**

Wedded to My Sword: The Revolutionary War Service of Light Horse Harry Lee **(2012)**

Cast Off the British Yoke: The Old Dominion and American Independence, 1763-1776 **(2014)**

A Universal Appearance of War: The Revolutionary War in Virginia, 1775-1781 **(2014)**

Acknowledgements

I am grateful to several people for their assistance with this book, beginning with Genevieve Bugay, the general manager of the Hugh Mercer Apothecary in Fredericksburg. Genevieve provided me access to the museum's files and kindly reviewed the manuscript. John Mills, the Resource Interpretive Specialist at the Princeton Battlefield State Park was generous with both his time and knowledge of the Battle of Princeton. I owe a big thank you to Debbie Riley of Heritage Books for her help with the maps and images in the book.

As always, I found the Simpson Library at the University of Mary Washington and the Rockefeller Library at Colonial Williamsburg very valuable resources. Lastly, I want to thank my wife, Sue, for continuing to support my passion for the American Revolution.

Chapter One

"Such Men as Col. Mercer… Would be of Great Service."

1726 – 1761

Hugh Mercer was born on January 16, 1726 at Pitsligo Manse, in northeast Scotland.[1] His father, William Mercer, was a Presbyterian minister. Little is known about Mercer's childhood, but as the son of a local church leader it is likely that his father provided him with a solid education. At the age of fourteen, Hugh Mercer was sent to Marischal College in Aberdeen where he studied Greek, Latin, Theology, Hebrew, Mathematics, Philosophy, and Physics.[2] His fourth year of study included Physical Science, Chemistry, and Medicine, all in preparation for a career in medicine.[3] Mercer completed his studies in the spring of 1744 at the age of eighteen.[4]

Mercer's activities over the next 18 months are uncertain; no records exist to explain his whereabouts or activities, but Malcolm Selkirk, a Scottish researcher with knowledge of Mercer's family history in Scotland, speculates that the young man returned home to Pitsligo and likely fell under the wing

---

[1] Malcolm G. Selkirk, *The Story of Hugh Mercer, Doctor, Soldier, and Jacobite,* Unpublished Manuscript, (Perthshire, Scotland: 1991), 14

[2] Ibid., 17

[3] Ibid., 18

[4] Ibid., 19

Scotland

Pitsligo
Fraserburgh
Culloden
Aberdeen
Leith
Edinburgh
Glasgow
Dumfries

of Dr. John Cruickshank of Fraserburgh.[5] Dr. Cruickshank had practiced medicine in the vicinity of Pitsligo since Mercer's birth and it makes sense that if Mercer did return home he would have welcomed an opportunity to learn the practice of medicine from such an experienced doctor and family acquaintance.

Jacobite Uprising

Within months of Mercer's likely return to Pitsligo, Scotland was ablaze with rebellion against the King of England. Prince Charles Edward Stuart, Bonnie Prince Charles to his supporters in Scotland, landed in Scotland in July to reclaim his throne, lost by his grandfather during the Glorious Revolution of 1688. Many of Scotland's leaders rallied to Charles Stuart's cause and young Hugh Mercer appears to have been swept up in the rebellion.

Records of Mercer's service in the Jacobite uprising are scarce, but researcher Malcolm Selkirk has concluded that 19 year old Hugh Mercer served in the local lord's troop of horse. Alexander Forbes, the 4th Baron Forbes of Pitsligo, answered Charles Stuart's call to serve and raised both cavalry and infantry for that purpose.[6] It is in this unit that Selkirk believes Mercer served as an assistant surgeon's mate, probably to Dr. Cruickshank.[7]

If Mercer did serve in Lord Pitsligo's regiment of horse, his service did not last a year, for in April 1746 the Scottish rebels met a much larger English army on the field of Culloden. Outnumbered almost two to one, the Scots had little chance

---

[5] Ibid.
[6] Ibid., 23
[7] Ibid., 24-26

and were routed in half an hour. Charles Stuart fled Scotland and his supporters scattered, many to be arrested and punished.

Hugh Mercer went into hiding and made his way to the coastal town of Leith, where he obtained passage on a ship to the American colonies and arrived in Philadelphia, Pennsylvania sometime in 1747.[8]

Mercer did not remain long in Philadelphia. Still fearful of arrest, the young fugitive made his way west, to the Conococheague settlements of Cumberland County, Pennsylvania. He likely found his medical knowledge in demand in such an isolated area and spent the next eight years on the Pennsylvania frontier.

French & Indian War

The advent of the French and Indian War in 1754 marked the beginning of a new phase in Mercer's life. This conflict erupted after a young colonial officer from Virginia named George Washington clashed with a combined French and Indian force about 50 miles southeast of present day Pittsburg and 85 miles west of Mercer's location in Cumberland County. The Battle of Fort Necessity helped ignite a global conflict with enormous consequences. Mercer did not participate in the fighting at Fort Necessity in 1754 or the much larger battle the following year (Braddock's Defeat) but he was swept up in the conflict soon after Braddock's Defeat.

General Edward Braddock's army of British and colonial troops, determined to secure the Ohio River Valley from French encroachment, blazed a road through the wilderness

---

[8] Ibid., 36-37

towards the Ohio River in the spring of 1755. As Braddock's advance guard approached French held Fort Duquesne (present day Pittsburg) they were ambushed by hundreds of Indians allied with the French. Braddock's men became disordered and fell back upon the main body, which in turn became disordered. The result was disaster for the British and their colonial brethren. Hundreds of Braddock's men, including the General himself, fell in what became a rout.

It is possible that Hugh Mercer treated some of the wounded survivors from Braddock's Defeat, but his military service did not officially begin until after General Braddock's army was destroyed in the Pennsylvania wilderness in 1755.

Emboldened by the defeat of General Braddock's British regulars and the colonial militia, Indian war parties allied with the French raided numerous Pennsylvania frontier settlements in the fall of 1755, sparking an outcry for help among the settlers. The pacifist sentiments of Pennsylvania's Quaker dominated government were forced aside and authorization was granted to form militia companies to defend the frontier and fight back. Twenty-nine year old Hugh Mercer was chosen to lead one of these militia companies from Cumberland County in late 1755. He was appointed the rank of captain.[9] By the spring of 1756, Mercer held a captain's commission in a different unit, the 2nd Battalion of the Pennsylvania Regiment of regulars.[10] These troops were recruited for continuous service (as opposed to the short enlistments of local militia) and were viewed as the best troops Pennsylvania had.

---

[9] Thomas Lynch Montgomery, ed. *Pennsylvania Archives*, Series 5, Vol. 1, (Harrisburg, PA: Harrisburg Publishing Company, 1906), 31
[10] Ibid.

6

Western Pennsylvania: 1759-1763

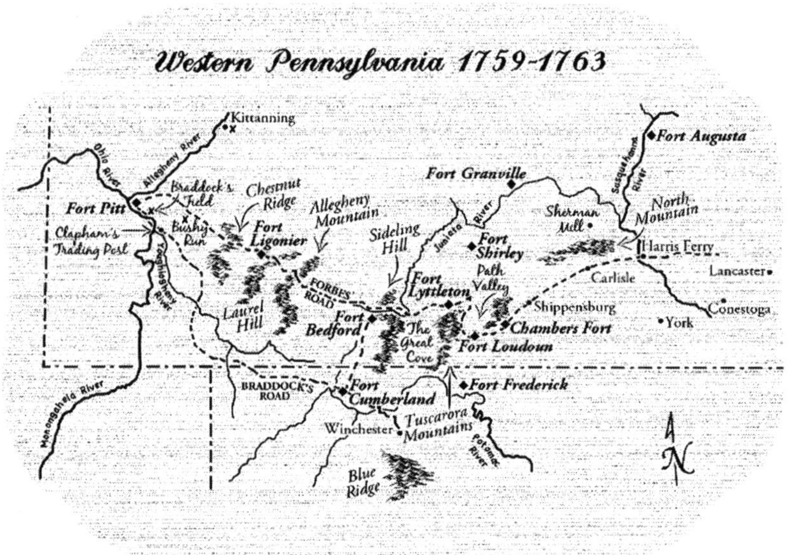

Source: Novel *Forbes Road* by Robert J. Shade
Artist: Stephen Templeton

In March of 1756, Captain Mercer found himself pulling double duty, commanding short term militia at Fort Shirley (35 miles west of the town of Carlisle) who were eager to return to their homes, while recruiting 60 men for his new company in the Pennsylvania Regiment.[11] Captain Mercer travelled to Carlisle in mid-April to recruit and described his challenge to Governor Robert Hunter Morris in a letter:

> *I am now about filling up my company to sixty men, agreeable to your orders, and have drawn upon the commissaries for thirty pounds for this purpose. A garrison of thirty men are now at Fort Shirley, engaged to remain there until the first of May, by which time I am in hopes of continuing the company and shall immediately thereupon repair thither. It is to be feared that our communication with the settlement will soon be cut off unless a greater force is ordered for the garrison.* [12]

Mercer explained that with so few troops currently garrisoning the fort, he was unable to send out patrols or even detachments to escort much needed supplies threatened by frequent Indian raids. Despite these challenges, however, Captain Mercer assured Governor Morris that he was pleased with his appointment:

---

[11] Thomas Lynch Montgomery, ed., *Report of the Commission to Locate The Site of the Frontier Forts of Pennsylvania*, Vol. 1, (Harrisburg, PA: Wm. Stanly Ray, State Printer, 1916), 571, 576-577

[12] Ibid. "Captain Mercer to Governor Morris, 18 April, 1756," 576-577

> *The trust your Honour has been pleased to repose in me, in giving me command of Fort Shirley, calls for my warm acknowledgements and cannot fail of engaging my utmost affection and zeal in the execution of your orders.*[13]

Unfortunately, the limited resources and troops available to defend Pennsylvania's frontier encouraged continued Indian raids into the summer. The fall of Fort Granville (25 miles northeast of Fort Shirley) in late July to a combined force of Indians and French stunned Pennsylvania authorities and prompted them to approve a strike against Kittanning, an Indian stronghold and staging area 30 miles northeast of French held Fort Duquesne (Pittsburg). It was hoped that this raid would also apprehend or kill a notorious Indian leader nicknamed Captain Jacob who was thought responsible for many of the raids on the Pennsylvania frontier.

Kittanning Expedition : 1756

Lieutenant-Colonel John Armstrong was selected to lead the 2nd Battalion of the Pennsylvania Regiment (approximately 300 men) against Kittanning. They spent most of August gathering the necessary supplies for the expedition. Captain Mercer's company participated in the expedition and departed Fort Shirley on August 30th, with the rest of Armstrong's 2nd Battalion.[14]

---

[13] Ibid.

[14] "Lieutenant Colonel Armstrong to Governor William Denny, 14 September, 1756," *Minutes of the Provincial Council of Pennsylvania,* Vol. 7, (Harrisburg: Theo. Fenn & Co., 1851), 257

After a seven day march, Lieutenant Colonel Armstrong determined that they were in striking distance of Kittanning. He deposited the provisions he needed for the return march amongst some trees, relieving both the packhorses and men of some of their burden, and pressed forward. Mercer and the rest of the expedition now carried just a day's worth of food in their pouches and haversacks.

Armstrong wanted to attack the Indian village at dawn, so he led his battalion forward after sunset to get into position. Around 10 p.m. his scouts reported a campfire ahead on the trail. Informed that only a handful of Indians were gathered around the fire, Armstrong considered rushing them, but he feared that one might escape into the darkness to warn the Indians at Kittanning, so he left 12 men under Lieutenant Hogg (along with the battalion's pack horses and their haversacks of food) to observe the sleeping Indians and attack them at dawn.[15] The rest of the battalion quietly backtracked and made a wide circuit around the Indian party.

The Pennsylvanians struggled in the dark over rough, wooded, terrain and eventually heard drums and singing, which guided them to the edge of Kittanning.[16] Hidden near a cornfield, Armstrong and his men settled down and waited for dawn. Many of Armstrong's men fell asleep while they waited, exhausted by the day's thirty mile march.[17]

Armstrong posted several small detachments on nearby hills overlooking the village and proceeded to attack at dawn with the rest of his force. He reported that

---

[15] Ibid., 258
[16] Ibid.
[17] Ibid., 259

> *The Attack was begun in the Corn Field, and the Men with all Expedition possible, dispatched thro' the several parts thereof; a party being also dispatched to the Houses, which were then discovered by the light of the Day.*[18]

The startled Indians, many of them asleep outdoors, scrambled for cover. Their leader, Captain Jacobs, was heard ordering the women and children to flee into the woods and his men to fight, exclaiming that, "*the White Men were at last come, they wou'd then have Scalps enough....*"[19]

Lieutenant Colonel Armstrong proudly recounted to his superiors that

> *Our Men with great Eagerness passed thro' and Fired in the Corn Field, where they had several Returns from the Enemy, as they also had from the Opposite side of the River.*[20]

Heavy musket fire from a few of the Indian buildings soon attracted the Pennsylvanians' attention and cost them several men. Lieutenant Colonel Armstrong ordered the buildings to be burned and soon the village was ablaze. Captain Jacobs had barricaded himself in a building and refused to surrender, announcing that, "*he was a Man and wou'd not be a Prisoner.*"[21] When the fire and smoke became too much to bear, the Indian leader bolted out of the house in a futile

---

[18] Ibid.
[19] Ibid.
[20] Ibid.
[21] Ibid., 260

attempt to escape. He, along with his wife and son, were shot down by the Pennsylvanians.[22]

Early in the attack, Captain Mercer was struck in the arm by a musket ball and taken to the top of a nearby hill where a tourniquet was applied to stop the bleeding.[23] Lieutenant Colonel Armstrong was also wounded in the battle, shot in the shoulder and assisted to a different hill for treatment.[24] Despite the loss of these officers, the battle continued and the fire spread. Stores of gunpowder in several buildings ignited, blowing buildings and people apart.

Armstrong, who despite his wound was still in command, learned from rescued English prisoners that Captain Jacobs expected to be joined by a party of Frenchmen that very day and together they were going to attack Fort Shirley. The prisoners also reported that a party of 24 Indians left Kittanning the day before in preparation of this attack.

Armstrong was disturbed to hear this and realized that the Indian party described by the prisoners was likely the one discovered the night before on the trail. If so, they outnumbered the small detachment that Armstrong left behind under Lieutenant Hogg. With virtually all of the battalion's packhorses in the care of Lieutenant Hogg, Armstrong feared that his expedition was in jeopardy. He explained to Governor Denny upon his return that

> *Our Provisions being...some thirty Miles back, except what were in the men's Haversacks, which were left with the Horses and Blankets with*

---

[22] Ibid.
[23] Ibid.
[24] Ibid.

> *Lieutenant Hogg and His party, and a Number of wounded People then on hand; by the Advice of the Officers it was thought imprudent then to wait for the cutting down the Corn Field (which was before designed), but immediately to collect our Wounded and force our March back in the best manner we cou'd wich we did by collecting a few Indian Horses to carry off our wounded*.[25]

In other words, Armstrong concluded that they had to leave Kittanning immediately to return to Lieutenant Hogg. Armstrong regretted that his early departure prevented the destruction of the corn field but he felt he had no choice, the battalion had to rush back to secure the provisions and horses left under Lieutenant Hogg's care.[26]

When Armstrong and the battalion commenced their return march, Captain Mercer was nowhere to be found. Armstrong was informed by some of Mercer's men that

> *Captain Mercer being wounded, was induced, as we have reason to believe, by some of his Men, to leave the main Body with his Ensign, John Scott, and ten or twelve Men, they being heard to tell him that we were in great Danger, and that they cou'd take him into the Road a nigh Way.*[27]

Robert Robinson, a participant in the expedition, gave a similar account of Mercer's disappearance:

---

[25] Ibid., 261
[26] Ibid.
[27] Ibid.

> *We were then preparing to leave the town, when captain Mercer, who had his right arm broke in the town; his company composed of traders, who persuaded their captain that there would not one living man of us ever get home, and if he, capt. Mercer would go with them they would take him to a near cut.*[28]

Mercer and this small party of men disappeared down a trail, but soon fell in with a party of Indians and scattered. Captain Mercer, who was on horseback with his broken arm in a sling, was accompanied by his ensign, John Scott, and a private, Thomas Burke.[29] Believing they had escaped the Indians, they proceeded down a road but had to stop to re-dress Mercer's wound. Weak from the loss of blood, Captain Mercer nearly fainted upon dismounting. Suddenly, the small party spotted an Indian approaching and Scott and Burke panicked. They mounted Captain Mercer's horse and, "*rode off, leaving* [Mercer] *to his fate*."[30] Despite his condition, Mercer acted quickly and, according to Robinson

> [Mercer] *lay down behind a log, it happening to be thick with weeds, the Indian came about six feet from him and seeing Burke and Scott riding, he gave out a halloo and ran after….*[31]

---

[28] Archibald Loudon, ed., "Narrative of Robert Robinson," *A Selection of Some of the most Interesting Narratives of Outrages Committed by the Indians in Their Wars with the White People,* Vol. 2, (Carlisle, PA, 1811), 163-64

[29] Ibid.

[30] Ibid.

[31] Ibid.

Captain Mercer carefully moved into a thicket and lay there until nightfall, after which he began a nearly two week journey through the Pennsylvania wilderness to reach Fort Littleton. Robinson claimed that

> *It was at the time of the plumbs being ripe, but that did not last long enough...all the food* [Mercer] *got after the plumbs were done was one rattle snake, and to eat it raw.*[32]

A similar account of Mercer's incredible ordeal appeared in the *New York Mercury* a few weeks after he reached Fort Littleton

> *We hear that Captain Mercer was 14 Days in getting to Fort Littleton. He had a miraculous Escape, living ten Days on two dried Clams and a Rattle Snake, with the Assistance of a few Berries. The Snake kept sweet for Several Days, and, coming near Fort Shirley, he found a piece of dry Beef, which our People had lost, and on Trial rejected it, because the Snake was better. His wounded Arm is in a good Way, tho' it could be but badly drest, and a Bone broke.*[33]

Robinson provided more detail of the final days of Mercer's journey, noting that at some point Mercer spotted another person at a distance who he feared was a hostile Indian. Relieved to discover it was one of his own men, the two starving and exhausted soldiers carried on. They

---

[32] Ibid.

[33] *New York Mercury*, 4 October, 1756, 1

eventually became so weak that they collapsed. Robinson claimed that

> *They...were not far from Franks town, when the soldier* [with Mercer] *lay down unable to go any further, with an intention never more to rise.*[34]

Mercer was unable to convince his companion to continue on, so he left him and struggled on alone. After seven miles, Captain Mercer, "*also lay down giving up all hopes of ever getting home.*" [35] But fortune shined of Captain Mercer and his companion; Mercer was discovered by a party of pro-British Cherokee Indians. He directed the Indians to his stricken comrade, who was also rescued, and both were taken to Fort Littleton where they slowly recovered.[36]

Lieutenant Colonel Armstrong and the rest of his battalion, including most of Mercer's company, had also made it back to Fort Littleton (despite the loss of Lieutenant Hogg and his detachment and the bulk of their provisions). The expedition, which tactically was only nominally successful given the high number of casualties (50) suffered by Armstrong, was a big success psychologically, boosting the morale of settlers throughout Pennsylvania.[37]

Within a month of his return, Captain Mercer was back with his company in the 2nd Battalion.[38] The next year was

---

[34] Loudon, ed., "Narrative of Robert Robinson," *A Selection of Some of the most Interesting Narratives of Outrages Committed by the Indians in Their Wars with the White People,* Vol. 2, 164

[35] Ibid.

[36] Ibid.

[37] Montgomery, ed. *Pennsylvania Archives*, Series 5, Vol. 1, 67-68

[38] Joseph Waterman, *With Sword and Lancet: The Life of General Hugh Mercer*, (Richmond, VA: Garrett and Massie, Inc., 1941), 31

rather uneventful for Captain Mercer. Indian raids along the Pennsylvania frontier diminished considerably after the Kittanning Raid (in part because of the raid but also because of negotiations between the British and several Indian tribes). The area also benefitted from the lack of British and French operations in Pennsylvania, their attention temporarily fixed elsewhere.

At the end of 1757 Mercer was promoted to Major and became a staff officer in the 2nd Battalion. As second in command of the battalion, (behind a new battalion commander, Lieutenant Colonel James Burd) Mercer's company level duties became battalion level duties. Mercer's friend and military mentor, Lieutenant Colonel Armstrong left the 2nd Battalion to assume command of the 1st Battalion. Above all of the officers was Governor William Denny, who served (on paper) as the regiment's commanding officer.[39]

Major Mercer remained posted at the forts west of the Susquehanna River into 1758. After a long lull in activity in Pennsylvania, the British decided to launch an expedition (in conjunction with expeditions in New York and Canada) against the French at Fort Duquesne . The expedition against Fort Duquesne was led by British General John Forbes, a Scotsman like Mercer, who had hundreds of colonial troops, bolstered by 1,200 Scottish Highlanders, at his disposal.[40]

---

[39] Montgomery, ed. *Pennsylvania Archives*, Series 5, Vol. 1, 98

[40] Francis Parkman, *Montcalm and Wolfe: The French and Indian War*, (New York: Barnes and Noble, 2005), 348
Originally published in 1884

Forbes Expedition : 1758

One of the biggest challenges for the British in capturing Fort Duquesne was moving a large army through the wilderness to attack it. Instead of following Braddock's road from Virginia, General Forbes chose a shorter route and decided to build a new road through Pennsylvania. He protected this new road, and the army building it, with a series of forts that were constructed along the road route. Construction of the road started in the summer of 1758 and proceeded into the fall.

In late May, Major Mercer was promoted to Lieutenant Colonel and placed in command of the Pennsylvania Regiment's 3rd Battalion. He spent the next six months assisting in the construction of what became known as the Forbes Road, shuttling men and supplies from Fort Littleton during the summer and from Raystown (Fort Bedford) during the fall, to the advance parties that were building and guarding the new road to Fort Duquesne. Mercer's duties brought him in frequent contact with Colonel George Washington, the commander of Virginia's 1st Regiment of colonial regulars. In fact, Mercer was posted with Washington at Raystown for much of the fall of 1758.

Although the construction of the road took much longer and was much harder than expected, General Forbes and his men steadily advanced westward. In mid-September, Forbes allowed an over eager Major James Grant to push ahead of the road with a force of approximately 800 Highlanders and colonial troops to reconnoiter Fort Duquesne. Grant reached the fort undetected but was too aggressive in his movements and provoked an attack from the French and their Indian allies that resulted in nearly 300 British casualties and his own capture.[41]

Despite this setback, the expedition continued westward, greatly aided by British diplomatic efforts with the Delaware, Shawnee, and Mingo Indians, all allies of the French. A peace agreement with these Indians was reached in October, and just like that, France's ability to hold Fort Duquesne, which was garrisoned with only 300 French militia) vanished.

General Forbes initially did not realize that most of the Indians around Fort Duquesne had abandoned the French in November. In fact, a war council held on November 11th, (in which Lieutenant Colonel Mercer was a participant) concluded that with winter fast approaching, it was best to halt their march to Fort Duquesne and resume in the spring.

Reports from three captives brought into camp a few days after the war council that Fort Duquesne was in a defenseless condition convinced General Forbes to change his mind.[42] He ordered a large infantry detachment forward to investigate. As this force neared Fort Duquesne they heard explosions. When they came within view of the fort, they found it in ruins. The French commander, realizing he had no chance to successfully defend Fort Duquesne, had fled with his men, burning the fort upon his departure.[43]

---

[41] Ibid., 358-60

[42] W.W. Abbot, ed., "Col. Washington to Francis Fauquier, 2 December, 1758," *The Papers of George Washington, Colonial Series,* Vol. 6, (Charlottesville: University Press of Virginia, 1988), 161

[43] Parkman, 361-62

Mercer Commands Fort Pitt

Lieutenant Colonel Mercer was not with the troops that first reached the ruins of Fort Duquesne. He arrived three weeks later from Fort Ligonier to assume command of the small garrison of Pennsylvania and Virginia provincials left behind to rebuild and secure the site through the winter. Mercer reported that

> *On my arrival here the 17th* [of December] *I found the works carrying on with great expedition, the Barracks being raisd & roofed & the Bastions almost inclosed. In a few days more the heaviest parts of our Work will be finish'd....*[44]

General Forbes had wished to maintain a much larger force at Pittsburg, (the new English name for the site) but, as Colonel Washington noted to Governor Fauquier in Virginia, "*the want of Provisions rendered it impossible to leave more than 200 men in all there.*"[45] As a result, a few days after Mercer arrived, General Forbes led the bulk of his army eastward, where it would be easier to supply them. Lieutenant Colonel Mercer and his 200 men were left behind to make due the best they could through the winter.

Colonel Washington feared for the garrison's safety, predicting that, "*Without peculiar exertion,* [Mercer] *must, I*

---

[44] S.K Stevens, Donald H. Kent, Autumn L. Leonard, eds., " Hugh Mercer to Bouquet, 19 December, 1758" *The Papers of Henry Bouquet*, Vol. 2, (Harrisburg: Pennsylvania Historical and Museum Commission, 1951), 635

[45] Abbot, ed., "Col. Washington to Francis Fauquier, 2 December, 1758," *The Papers of George Washington, Colonial Series,* Vol. 6, 161

fear, abandon the place – or perish," if attacked by the French over the winter.[46] Such a possibility of attack was a constant threat to Mercer and his small garrison and they worked hard to erect defensive works as fast as they could.

Lieutenant Colonel Mercer also spent a significant amount of time treating with the scores of Indians who gathered at Pittsburg. Mercer realized that it was essential to maintain good relations with Britain's new allies. He discovered, however, that their demands for trade goods and provisions (particularly flour of which the fort was almost out) was difficult to satisfy. Mercer complained to Colonel Henry Bouquet, a British officer whom Mercer would have frequent contact with, that

> *Our new Allies being extremely sollicitous for larger supplies of* [flour] *than I can afford* [have] *become very troublesome, having been indulged in too many of their extravagant Demands before my Arrival, And their Expectations raised too high.*[47]

Mercer added that an interpreter would go a long way towards improving communication with the Indians.

In January, the steady stream of Indian delegations that arrived at Pittsburg to meet with Mercer strained the garrison's supply of provisions. On January 8th, 1759 Mercer informed Colonel Bouquet that

---

[46] Ibid.

[47] Stevens, Kent, and Leonard, eds., " Hugh Mercer to Bouquet, 19 December, 1758," *The Papers of Henry Bouquet*, Vol. 2, 635

> *For these five or six days , we have entertained here upwards of a hundred and fifty Indians. As One Party goes and another Comes. It is not in my power to prevent an Extravagant Consumption of Provisions.*[48]

Fortunately for Mercer and his men, relief supplies arrived by horseback before provisions ran out.

As the winter passed, Mercer's concern about a French counterstroke against Fort Pitt eased, thanks in part to a reinforcement of 200 Scottish Highlanders who arrived in late January.[49] Provisions remained tight for many more weeks, but the garrison persevered and safely passed the winter.

Lieutenant Colonel Mercer's efforts at Fort Pitt attracted the notice of the highest ranks of the British army. In March, British General Jeffrey Amherst, the ranking British officer in North America, expressed confidence in Lieutenant Colonel Mercer's, "*Zeal and attachment to the Kings Service and his Judgement and alacrity in executing whatever may tend to the Honour of His Majesty's arms*." [50] Amherst wished Mercer to know that he had permission to act offensively against the enemy should the opportunity arise. Upon learning of Amherst's comments from Colonel Bouquet, Mercer, the former Scottish rebel in hiding, replied

---

[48] Donald H. Kent, Louis M. Waddell, Autumn L. Leonard, eds., " Mercer to Bouquet, 8 January, 1759", *The Papers of Henry Bouquet*, Vol. 3, (Harrisburg: Pennsylvania Historical and Museum Commission, 1976), 24

[49] Ibid., " Mercer to Bouquet, 29 January, 1759," 93

[50] Ibid., "Amherst to Bouquet, 5 March 1759," 174

His Excellency Genl Amherst may rest Assured, no opportunity of annoying the Enemy, this Way, will be omitted; and that any Enterprize that appears equal to our Force, will be entered upon by the Officers & Soldiers of this Garrison, with a Zeal & Alacrity becoming those, who possess a share of that ardour, which, at this glorious era, universally animates the subjects of His Majestie.[51]

A change in command among the British troops in Pennsylvania occurred in March when General Forbes succumbed to a long illness in Philadelphia and died. His replacement, General John Stanwix, arrived in Philadelphia in late March and for a moment it appeared that Mercer's immediate superior, Colonel Henry Bouquet, with whom Mercer had developed a strong admiration and friendship, was to be replaced. Mercer wrote an affectionate letter to Bouquet in response to Bouquet's expected departure:

Your letter...gave me, I must own, a sensible Concern, as it seemed to hint at your removal from this frontier. I cannot easily relinquish the hopes I had flattered myself with of passing another Campaign under your Command, and experiencing repeated Instances of Candour & indulgence to small errors; The memory of these will however, remain, and tho my letters may not pursue & persecute you, yet a thousand warm, tho Silent Wishes, for your honour & happiness will never be wanting.[52]

---

[51] Ibid., " Mercer to Bouquet, 21 March, 1759," 213
[52] Ibid., " Mercer to Bouquet, 4 April, 1759," 232

Mercer's letter proved premature as General Stanwix chose to keep Colonel Bouquet at his post in Pennsylvania.

At the end of March, Lieutenant Colonel Mercer attempted to fulfill General Amherst's desire for offensive action against the French in western Pennsylvania by launching a strike against Venango, a small French settlement and fort at the confluence of the Allegheny River and French Creek, about 70 miles north of Pittsburg. Mercer marched north from Fort Pitt with 200 troops on March 25th.[53] Another 50 men in ten bateaus loaded with provisions and supplies proceeded upriver with orders to join Mercer at Venango as soon as they could.[54] Unfortunately for the expedition, heavy rain flooded the river and delayed the bateaus; after three days they had only proceeded 20 miles upriver.[55] The supply boats came under fire from both banks of the river on March 28th, and the detachment's commander, Captain Clayton, sought the safety of an island in the middle of river. An account of the incident appeared in the *Pennsylvania Gazette*:

> *All of the Men, in one of the Battoes, were killed or wounded; the others pushed to an island, where they landed, and heard Hooping and Firing of Guns on both Sides of the River; this, with the Height of the Waters, obliged them to return, and left one Battoe, with 5 Men.* [On March] *30th the Battoe came floating down the River, with 5 Men in it, all scalped, one of them was alive, when we took up the Battoe, and lived some Hours. An Express was sent* [to] *Colonel*

---

[53] "Extract from a Letter from Pittsburgh, dated April 2," *Pennsylvania Gazette*, 3 May, 1759, 3

[54] Ibid.

[55] Ibid.

> [Mercer] *to inform him of Captain Clayton's Disaster. The Express overtook* [Mercer] *45 Miles from* [Pittsburg], *where he was stopped by the Waters being so high, and was obliged to return....*[56]

Colonel Mercer was undoubtedly displeased by these events, but without the extra provisions and supplies in the batteau, he was powerless to continue with the expedition.

Just two weeks later, Colonel Mercer was instructed to curtail offensive operations in preparation for a summer expedition on the Ohio:

> *You are not to attempt anything more upon the Enemy's Posts up the River till you receive new directions for it, as a Check in the Circumstances could be attended with great Risk, but you are to remain upon the defensive, and keep a good Look out besides your Spies to be able to defeat any Enterprise of the Enemy against your Fort or Ligonier.*[57]

While Mercer waited for further instructions, he scouted the area around Pittsburg for better defensible terrain to build an even larger fort and dutifully reported his findings to Colonel Bouquet and General Stanwix. Although the supply of provisions fell critically low (so low that horsemeat had to be used to feed the men) Mercer reported that the health of the troops improved daily with the change of season.[58] Small skirmishes occasionally erupted outside Fort Pitt between

---

[56] Ibid.

[57] Kent, Waddell,, and Leonard, eds., " Bouquet to Mercer, 13 April, 1759," *The Papers of Henry Bouquet*, Vol. 3, 240

[58] Ibid, " Mercer to Bouquet, 12 May, 1759," 277

parties of hostile Indians and detachments sent out by Mercer, but they were of no significance and did not threaten the garrison.

Frequent Indian reports of French preparations for an attack on Fort Pitt, however, kept Mercer and his garrison on edge well into the summer. He received a strong vote of confidence from his superior, Colonel Bouquet, on June 1st, 1759:

> *This is a Critical time for you but we confide entirely in your Prudence and Industrious to extraicate yourself from the difficulties that surround you.*[59]

Bouquet added that help was on the way.

While Mercer waited for reinforcements (and much needed provisions), he held an Indian conference in July to encourage more support from them. Mercer considered the meeting a success, claiming that, "*it gave general satisfaction to them,*" but confessed that, "*their force is too small, to be of consequence on this Occasion.*"[60]

The occasion Mercer referred to was the apparent impending French attack upon Pittsburg. Indian reports claimed that a large French and Indian force, with numerous cannon, had gathered north of Pittsburg and planned to attack either Fort Pitt or Fort Ligonier (or perhaps both).[61] Mercer was confident that he could defend Pittsburg, but expressed concern for an expected supply convoy from Fort Ligonier. "*I am in hopes* [the enemy] *are not in a Situation to insult it upon*

---

[59] Ibid., " Bouquet to Mercer, 1 June, 1759," 358
[60] Ibid., "Mercer to Bouquet, 11 July, 1759, 399
[61] Ibid.

the Road," wrote Mercer.[62] He added that upon the convoy's arrival his force at Pittsburg would number "*near 1,000 strong*," and would welcome the chance to defend the post against any attackers.

As it turned out, Mercer's determination was not tested. The French troops meant for an attack on Fort Pitt were diverted at the last minute for a futile attempt to relieve Fort Niagara, the embattled French fortress on Lake Erie. The lynchpin of France's Ohio Valley land holdings through which supplies and trade goods for their outposts and the Indians flowed, Fort Niagara succumbed to a three week siege by the British in late July. The loss of Fort Niagara crippled France's ability to hold onto its forts in western Pennsylvania.

Mercer noticed a dramatic shift away from support of the French from among the Indians even before Fort Niagara fell. He reported to Colonel Bouquet on July 22nd, that

> *A happy oppertunity offers itself just now of clearing the Ohio intirely of French Men, Their Indians are wavering to a Man, & many drop off from them dayly, & will be fixed in the British Interest, by pursuing the Generals Plan of indulging them in a few Presents, and laying open a fair Trade.*[63]

Mercer offered a similar assessment to General Stanwix, declaring that, "*We have the Indians from Vinango* [Fort Machault] *abandoning the French and coming in to accept the Proposals made to them.*"[64]

---

[62] Ibid.
[63] Ibid., " Mercer to Bouquet, 22 July, 1759," 437
[64] Ibid., " Mercer to Stanwix, 22 July, 1759," 440

General Stanwix reacted to the good fortune of the British by proposing that Mercer's garrison at Fort Pitt be reduced to 350 men.[65] Stanwix wanted to create a surplus of supplies at Fort Pitt, but the supply wagons that delivered the provisions via Forbes's road were stretched to their limit and barely able to maintain the present garrison and the numerous Indians gathered at Pittsburg. The only way to build up a stockpile was to reduce the number of mouths to feed at Fort Pitt, so a large portion of Mercer's garrison was transferred out.

This move failed to account for the large amount of provisions consumed by the Indians in the effort to win them over to the British side. On August 10th, Colonel Bouquet complained, on behalf of General Stanwix, to George Croghan (an Indian trader and interpreter at Fort Pitt) that the situation with the Indians was no longer tolerable and had to change:

> *All the Indians upon the Communication cannot be more hurtfull to us than our pretended friends are in destroying our Provisions at Pittsburgh. The Consequences are the same, as it is Equal if the Convoys are destroyed upon the Road, or devoured by them at Pittsburgh. The King's orders are to build a Fort there which cannot be Effected without a large body of Men, and it is not possible to Send them as long as all the Provisions forwarded are daily consumed by that Idle People: They have had full time to come to a determination, and this can Subsist no longer upon this footing: We cannot Subsist a great number of them and form a Magazine for the Troops: Therefore The General desires that You put*

[65] Ibid., " Stanwix to Byrd, 23 July, 1759," 449

> *an End to that useless Consumption; which is our evident ruin.*[66]

Colonel Bouquet sent similar instructions to Lieutenant Colonel Mercer on the same day. Mercer struggled to comply, admitting to Bouquet that

> *As to the expence of Provisions upon Indians I regret it extreamly, but freely acknowledge it above my ability to keep fair with them and be more saving.*[67]

General Stanwix discovered firsthand the challenges Mercer faced in dealing with the Indians at Pittsburg upon his arrival in late August.

General Stanwix's primary mission at Pittsburg was to establish an impregnable post to preserve and project British power in western Pennsylvania and beyond. Construction of a new, stronger fort began in September and dominated the activities of Lieutenant Colonel Mercer and the garrison for the rest of the fall. Mercer, relieved of the responsibility of command, declared to Governor Denny in mid-September that

> *A perfect tranquility reigns here since General Stanwix arrived, the works of the new fort go on briskly, and no Enemy appears near the Camp or upon the Communication.*[68]

---

[66] Ibid., "Bouquet to Croghan, 10 August, 1759," 531

[67] Ibid., "Mercer to Bouquet, 15 August, 1759," 565

[68] Samuel Hazard, ed., "Col. Mercer to Gov. Denny, 15 September, 1759," *Pennsylvania Archives*, Series 1, Vol. 3, (Philadelphia: Joseph Severns, Co., 1853), 685

General Stanwix was clearly impressed with Lieutenant Colonel Mercer and spoke highly of him in a letter to General Amherst in December. Amherst, who had occasionally communicated with Mercer during the past campaign, agreed with Stanwix's assessment of Mercer, replying that

> *Some such men as Col. Mercer amongst the Provincials would be of great Service, what you say of him does him great honour, & I shall be glad of any occasion to shew him any mark of Favour in my Power to Convince him of the Regard I have to your Recommendation. I think the Provincials are lucky in their Cols, for those I had the pleasure of having with me are really men of Merit & better officers in their Posts by much than any other Rank in the Regiments.*[69]

British victories at Fort Niagara and then Quebec City in 1759 significantly swung the war in Great Britain's favor and hampered the activities of the French and their remaining Indian allies in the west. The Pennsylvania Assembly concluded that was time to cut costs, and despite appeals from General Stanwix and other British military leaders, reduced their forces to just 150 officers and men over the winter.[70] Although Lieutenant Colonel Mercer retained his commission and remained on duty in the field, the Pennsylvania Regiment was reduced and restructured accordingly.

---

[69] Louis Waddell, John Tottenham, and Donald Kent, eds., " Amherst to Stanwix, 18 December, 1759," *The Papers of Henry Bouquet*, Vol. 4, (Harrisburg : Pennsylvania Historical and Museum Commission, 1978), 369

[70] Waterman, 37

In the spring of 1760 the Pennsylvania Assembly, believing that the war was winding down, decided to restore just two of the three battalions that had served to date. Colonel Mercer was appointed to command the 2nd Battalion. Mercer's friend and former commander, Colonel James Burd, led the 1st Battalion.[71]

Colonel Mercer spent the spring of 1760 one hundred and fifty miles to the east of Pittsburg at Fort Augusta on the Susquehanna River.[72] His experience at Fort Pitt was put to good use in negotiations with a delegation of Mingo Indians over the construction of a new road from Fort Augusta.[73]

Mercer was back at Fort Pitt by the summer, where he fell under the command of General Robert Monckton, General Stanwix's replacement. In July, Mercer led his battalion, 150 strong, north from Pittsburg to support Colonel Bouquet, who had marched ahead of Mercer with 500 troops towards Presque Isle (one of the abandoned French forts on Lake Erie).[74] Four hundred of Bouquet's troops were to continue by boats on Lake Erie (sent by General Amherst) to Fort Niagara, while the remainder, made up of Virginians, would remain to rebuild the fort at Presque Isle.[75]

With Bouquet's detachment of Virginians was Colonel Mercer's future brother-in-law, Lieutenant George Weedon of Fredericksburg, Virginia. Weedon and his fellow Virginians struggled mightily through the Pennsylvania woods to Presque Isle. Bouquet reported to General Monckton that

---

[71] Montgomery, ed. *Pennsylvania Archives*, Series 5, Vol. 1, 313
[72] Waterman, 58
[73] Ibid., 59
[74] Waddell, Tottenham, and Kent, eds. "Order of March, 7 July 1760," *The Papers of Henry Bouquet*, Vol.4, 623-24
[75] Ibid., "Bouquet to Peters, 18 July, 1760," 647

> *No Body without exception knows anything of the Country, or distances, except the Indians, who have been constantly drunk. The Path is very narrow full of fallen Trees, and requires many repairs to make it passable. The Pack Horses having no saddles, and some no saggings their loads are continually tumbling down, and tho' we march from morning to night, halting only at Noon, we make very little Way, as we must keep together.*[76]

Lieutenant Weedon described the expedition with much more humor once they reached Presque Isle.

> *I am at this time Commander in Chief of a Bullock Guard kept on an Island 6 miles long and about 4 miles broad, and Expect (from Indian Intelligence) to be attackd within 3 hours, but as the information comes from that fraternity my hand don't shake so much as it would from anyone Else. My Only Enemy, as yet has been the Musketoes, which have Surrounded me, flankt me, attack'd me in Front & Rear, but by the help of a little Smoke I as yet Keep my Ground.*[77]

Colonel Mercer joined Colonel Bouquet at Presque Isle with his battalion on July 18th, and was warmly greeted. For the next four months he and Colonel Bouquet worked to

---

[76] Ibid., "Bouquet to Monckton, 9 July, 1760," 625

[77] Harry M. Ward, *Duty, Honor or Country: General George Weedon and the American Revolution*, (Philadelphia: American Philosophical Society, 1979), 18

secure the site. One of the biggest challenges was keeping the men provisioned. The trip overland from Pittsburg was long and arduous, but supplies at Fort Niagara were limited, so neither fort could be counted on to provide enough provisions for the troops at Presque Isle. Along with the endless struggle to keep the detachment supplied came occasional skirmishes with hostile Indians, some from as far away as Detroit. The hard service on limited rations took a toll on Mercer and his men, but their spirits lifted considerably in October upon word of the fall of Montreal and surrender of all of Canada to General Amherst.

With the enlistments of his Pennsylvania troops due to expire in November and the war essentially ended in North America, Colonel Mercer realized that his service in the military was likely at an end. He returned to Fort Pitt in November and reluctantly received his discharge from the Pennsylvania Regiment in January 1761. In response, Colonel Mercer bid farewell to Pennsylvania and set out to start fresh in Virginia. It was time to resume his practice in medicine, and he was advised by some of the Virginians that he had met over the course of the war that Fredericksburg, a growing tobacco town upon the Rappahannock River in northern Virginia, was just the place for him to prosper.

Chapter Two

"[To Sacrifice] His Private Interest to the Service of His Country."

1761 – 1775

It appears that Hugh Mercer had only been in Fredericksburg for a little while when he penned a letter to his friend, Colonel Henry Bouquet to inform him of his activities.

> *Dear Sir,*
> *From many instances of your friendly concern for me, I cannot doubt of your receiving favourably some account of my situation: indeed the state of uncertainty I was for some time in with regard to business made me defer writing before now....all Prospect from the Pennsylvania Service failing I determined upon applying myself to the Practise of Physick, and this Place* [Fredericksburg] *was recommended as likely to afford a genteel subsistance in that Way. Whether it will answer my expectation I cannot yet judge; but from the reception I met with from the Gentlemen here, have reason to imagine it worthy a few months trial.*[1]

---

[1] Louis Waddell, John Tottenham and Donald Kent, eds., "H. Mercer to Bouquet, 12 February, 1761," *The Papers of Henry Bouquet*, Vol. 5, (Harrisburg : Pennsylvania Historical and Museum Commission, 1984), 290

Fredericksburg was a prosperous little town along the western bank of the Rappahannock River. John Harrower, an English tutor who arrived in Fredericksburg in 1774, described the town thirteen years after Mercer's arrival:

> [The] *principall street is about half an English Mile long, the houses generally at a little distance one from another, some of them being built of wood and some of them of brick, and all covered with wood made in the form of slates about four Inches broad... In the Toun the Church, the Counsell house, the Tolbooth, the Gallows & the Pillary are all within 130 yds. of each other. The Market house is a large brick building a little way from the Church.*[2]

When Mercer arrived in the winter of 1761, many of the residents of Fredericksburg were in the care of Dr. John Sutherland, a Scotsman like Mercer with a remarkably similar story. Sutherland trained in medicine in Scotland before his arrival in Virginia in 1748, (perhaps for the same reason Mercer sailed to the colonies) and settled down to practice the profession in Fredericksburg. He soon became very successful and prosperous, purchasing several lots in town and land outside of it.[3]

It is very likely that upon Mercer's arrival in Fredericksburg in 1761, Mercer made an immediate acquaintance of Sutherland. The two Scotsmen likely shared

---

[2] Edward Miles Riley, ed., "May 13, 1774," *The Journal of John Harrower: An Indentured Servant in the Colony of Virginia, 1773-1776*, (Williamsburg, VA: Colonial Williamsburg, Inc., 1963), 38

[3] Paula S. Felder, *Fielding Lewis and the Washington Family: A Chronicle of 18th Century Fredericksburg*, (The American History Company, 1998), 87-88

stories of home as well as their experiences in the medical profession. Although Dr. Sutherland and Dr. Mercer might have been competitors, it is also possible they became associates. Whatever the arrangement, Dr. Mercer was back to practicing medicine, and in 1762 he took on the responsibility of treating hundreds of new soldiers who were raised and quartered in Fredericksburg.[4]

The House of Burgesses had disbanded Virginia's provincial regiment from the French and Indian war in March 1762. There appeared to be no need for such troops once the French abandoned Canada. A request from British authorities for Virginia to maintain troops in the field until peace in Europe was finalized, however, was honored by Governor Francis Fauquier and the House of Burgesses just a month later in April, and the new recruits mustered in Fredericksburg.[5]

Dr. Mercer treated many of these soldiers, scores of who contracted smallpox. His services spanned from April to October and involved administering a large amount of medicine to the troops, for which he was only partially compensated by the House of Burgesses.[6] The regiment remained in Fredericksburg until December and then disbanded, the House of Burgesses refusing to reauthorize it

---

[4] John Pendleton Kennedy, ed. "9 December, 1762," *Journals of the House of Burgesses of Virginia, 1761-1765*, (Richmond, VA, 1908), 142

[5] George Reese, ed., "Governor Fauquier to Jeffrey Amherst, 7 April, 1762, and 21 June, 1762," *The Official Papers of Francis Fauquier, Lt. Gov. of Virginia,* Vol. 2, (Charlottesville, VA: Virginia Historical Society, 1981), 709 and 759

[6] Kennedy, ed. "9 December, 1762," *Journals of the House of Burgesses of Virginia, 1761-1765*, 142

for 1763.[7] They saw no need for the regiment thanks to reports of peace agreements being reached in Europe. The war had come to a close.

Mercer Decides to Stay

When Dr. Mercer first arrived in Fredericksburg, it was for a trial basis, to determine whether it was the place he wanted to settle in. He joined the Masonic Lodge during his first year in town and remained busy with the sick troops, but it wasn't until 1763 and his acquaintance with Isabella Gordon that his roots took hold in Fredericksburg.[8]

Isabella was the daughter of John and Margaret Gordon. John Gordon owned several lots in town, one of which had a tavern which he operated until his death in 1750. Mrs. Gordon continued to operate the tavern after her husband passed away and in 1764 George Weedon took on its management after he married Mrs. Gordon's other daughter, Catherine.[9]

There is some uncertainty to the actual date of Hugh Mercer's marriage to Isabella, but it appears to be close to the same time that George Weedon married Catherine, probably in 1763. Mercer and Weedon, now brothers-in-law, quickly became close friends and partners. The pair won three town lots together in a lottery in 1764 and over the next decade Mercer was the most frequent visitor to Weedon's tavern.[10]

---

[7] Reese, ed., "Governor Fauquier to Jeffrey Amherst, 15 December,1762," *The Official Papers of Francis Fauquier, Lt. Gov. of Virginia,* Vol. 2, 854

[8] Felder, 89

[9] Ward, 22-23

[10] Felder, 89

Dr. Mercer and Isabella settled in Fredericksburg and moved into the former residence of Dr. John Sutherland in 1766. Dr. Sutherland died in 1765 and had rented a house near the center of town on lot 50, (the corner of Amelia and Princess Anne Streets) from James Hunter. Mercer purchased the lot from Hunter for $480 pounds in 1766 and rented an adjoining building (lot 49) upon Caroline Street (the main street in Fredericksburg) to use for his medical practice.[11]

Dr. Mercer's Medical Practice

It is likely that Mercer assumed the care of many of Dr. Sutherland's patients and soon developed a thriving practice in Fredericksburg. When Jack Custis, Colonel Washington's young stepson, became ill in Caroline County while boarding at Johnathan Boucher's residence in July 1768 for his schooling, Dr. Mercer was mentioned by both Boucher and Washington as the person to consult.[12] Just a few months later, Dr. Mercer paid a visit to Mount Vernon, apparently to consult with another doctor regarding the poor health of Colonel Washington's step daughter, Patsy, who suffered from frequent seizures. Mercer stayed two nights at Mount Vernon, for which Washington paid him six pounds for his services.[13]

---

[11] Ibid.

[12] W.W. Abbot and Dorothy Twohig, eds., " *The Papers of George Washington, Colonial Series*, Vol. 8, (Charlottesville: University Press of Virginia, 1993), 116, 120

[13] Donald Jackson, ed., " January 30 to February 1769," *The Diaries of George Washington,1766-70,* Vol. 2 (Charlottesville: University Press of Virginia, 1976), 122-123, 126

The following year, 1770, Patsy Custis became gravely ill while accompanying her mother and Colonel Washington on a visit to Ferry Farm, the home of Washington's mother. Dr. Mercer was promptly summoned from across the river in Fredericksburg and treated Patsy. She remained under his care for nine days until it was determined safe to proceed back home to Mount Vernon.[14]

In 1771, Dr. Mercer entered a partnership with Dr. Ewen Clements. They announced the news in the Virginia Gazette:

> *Fredericksburg, May 28, 1771*
>
> *The Subscribers this Day became Partners in the Practice of PHYSICK and SURGERY, and have opened a Shop on the main Street, opposite to Mr. Henry Mitchell's Store, furnished with a large Assortment of DRUGS and MEDICINES of the best Quality, just imported from London, where Gentlemen of the Profession, and others, may be supplied at easy Rates, for ready Money.*[15]

The arrangement between Mercer and Clement called for Dr. Mercer to receive two thirds of the profits, something that may have troubled his partner for in a little over a year the partnership was dissolved.[16]

Dr. Mercer immediately formed a new partnership with John Jullian and once again advertised the news in the gazette:

---

[14] Ibid., "31 July, 1770," 257

[15] Alexander Purdie, *Virginia Gazette*, 6 June, 1771, 3

[16] Felder, 90 and Purdie and Dixon, *Virginia Gazette*, "6 August, 1772," 2

Fredericksburg, July1, 1772

The Subscribers have entered into Partnership in the Practice of PHYSICK and SURGERY, and keep their Shop next Door to Mrs. Julian's Tavern. They have on Hand a large Assortment of MEDICINES, largely imported, and intend to import, twice a year, Drugs of the best Quality, to be sold at reasonable Rates.[17]

Mercer's practice, which had already been strong, thrived under this new arrangement. A look at his ledger book for the years 1771-1773 shows over a hundred patients and 243 accounts.[18] Business was so strong that in 1774 Dr. Mercer made arrangements with Colonel Washington to purchase Ferry Farm, the 600 acre boyhood home of Washington. Colonel Washington's mother had recently moved into Fredericksburg and the farm sat empty, planted with corn and wheat, but uninhabited. Dr. Mercer offered Washington three pounds an acre, or 1800 pounds for the tract of land.[19] Washington asked for 2,000 pounds total, and Mercer agreed to pay that, with interest, over five years:

The Terms of Two Thousand Pounds will suit me at five Annual payments – I expect to discharge the Debt sooner, but as you are willing to let the money remain in my hands on Interest – will accept of that Indulgence….[20]

---

[17] Alexander Purdie and John Dixon, *Virginia Gazette*, "9 July, 1772," 3

[18] Felder, 90 and Dr. Hugh Mercer's Ledger Book 1771-73 on microfilm at the Simpson Library of the University of Mary Washington

[19] Beverly H. Runge, ed., "From Hugh Mercer, 21 March, 1774," *The Papers of George Washington, Colonial Series,* Vol. 10, (Charlottesville: University Press of Virginia, 1995), 2

[20] Ibid., "From Hugh Mercer, 6 April, 1774," 23

Dr. Mercer acquired other property holdings, both locally and on the frontier during his time in Fredericksburg.[21] He figured he would need such investments for his growing family, now up to four children by 1774.

Mercer's Children

Adversity struck the Mercer family in the case of their children as two of Dr. Mercer's sons (William and George) were born deaf. This kind of disability presented significant challenges to families in the 18th century, but Dr. Mercer, his wife, and their children seem to have handled the challenges well.

Surprisingly, the order of birth among the Mercer children remains unclear, no reliable source exists to provide birthdates, but it appears that William Mercer was born in 1765, followed by, Ann, the Mercer's only daughter, then two more sons, George Weedon Mercer and John Mercer. A fifth child, Hugh Tenant Weedon Mercer, would come in August 1776 while General Mercer was away in New Jersey during the Revolutionary War.

Political Unrest

In addition to balancing the demands of a house full of young children (two with special needs) and a thriving medical practice, Dr. Mercer found himself drawn deeper and deeper into the political issues of the day. As both a prominent doctor and resident of Fredericksburg, Dr. Mercer had frequent contact with Fredericksburg's political elite.

---

[21] Hugh Mercer's Will, *Spotsylvania County Records, Will Book E, 1772-1798*, 169

Although a Scot and a Presbyterian, (neither of which were typically embraced by native Virginians) Mercer was accepted into the ruling circles of Fredericksburg's society.

Mercer's role in the early protests over the Stamp Act and Townshend Duties was apparently minimal; his first participation of any note occurred on December 14th, 1774 when he was named as one of 45 members of a committee in Spotsylvania County to enforce the provisions of the Continental Association passed a few weeks earlier by the Continental Congress in Philadelphia.[22] The following day this new committee adopted a more militant stance against British policies (the Intolerable Acts, which punished Massachusetts for the Boston Tea Party). The Committee recommended that the people of Spotsylvania County

> *Raise Independent Companies of publick spirited Gentlemen to be ready on all occasions to defend this Colony and to act in Conjunction with the Independent Companies of the other Counties when it shall be judged most necessary....*[23]

Just two months earlier in Philadelphia, the Continental Congress had rejected a similar measure supported by Virginians Patrick Henry and Richard Henry Lee and had opted instead for economic sanctions to oppose Parliament's unconstitutional treatment of Massachusetts. Several Virginia counties believed that economic measures were an insufficient

---

[22] Robert L. Scribner, ed., "Spotsylvania County Committee, 14 December, 1774," *Revolutionary Virginia: The Road to Independence,* Vol. 2, (Charlottesville, VA: University Press of Virginia, 1975), 195

[23] Ibid., "Spotsylvania County Committee, 15 December, 1774," 196-197

response to Parliament so they formed their own independent militia companies, extra-legal bodies that were not authorized or recognized by Virginia's Royal Governor, John Murray, the Earl of Dunmore. The decision of the Spotsylvania County committee in mid-December to recommend that its citizens create similar independent militia companies placed Spotsylvania in this small, but growing group of militant Virginia counties.

The Spotsylvania committee selected eight men to, "*draw up proper Regulations for the forming of such Companies to be laid before the next monthly meeting.*"[24] Dr. Hugh Mercer was one of the eight selected, no doubt due to his extensive military experience in the French and Indian War. By February 1775, at least one such independent company existed in Spotsylvania County, for Nicholas Cresswell, a British traveler passing through Fredericksburg, observed the militia company exercise in town. He was not impressed, noting in his journal that, "*They make a poor appearance.*"[25]

In late March of 1775, Virginia's political leaders, minus Lord Dunmore, met in Richmond as a special convention to select and instruct Virginia's delegation to the 2nd Continental Congress. Patrick Henry proposed that the Convention adopt a resolution calling on all of Virginia's counties to place themselves in a posture of defense. An intense debate erupted; almost half of those in attendance viewed Henry's resolution as too provocative towards Britain. They urged less forceful measures to oppose Parliament. Henry's stirring words of, "Give Me Liberty or Give Me Death", however, won the

---

[24] Ibid., 197

[25] Nicholas Cresswell, *The Journal of Nicholas Cresswell,* (NY: Dial Press, 1974), 56

argument and the 2nd Virginia Convention adopted his resolution on March 23, 1775.

> *Resolved, that a well regulated Militia composed of Gentlemen and Yeomen is the natural Strength and only Security of a free Government: that such Militia in this Colony would forever render it unnecessary for the Mother Country to keep among us for the purpose of our Defense any standing Army of mercenary Forces, always subversive of the Quiet, and dangerous to the Liberties of the People.... Resolved therefore that this Colony be immediately put into a posture of Defense and that...a Committee to prepare a Plan for embodying, arming and disciplining such a Number of Men as may be sufficient for that purpose* [be formed].[26]

Over the next few weeks several county committees responded to Henry's resolution by forming their own independent militia companies, but many others still delayed; not everyone shared the sense of urgency that Patrick Henry and his supporters felt.

Williamsburg Powder Magazine

This changed on April 21st, 1775 when a detachment of British Marines and sailors from the *H.M.S. Magdalen*, anchored in the James River, seized barrels of gunpowder in the middle of the night from the powder magazine in Williamsburg. Governor Dunmore, alarmed by the actions of

[26] Scribner, ed., "Second Virginia Convention Proceedings, 23 March, 1775" *Revolutionary Virginia: The Road to Independence,* Vol. 2, 366-367

the 2nd Virginia Convention as well as by counties like Spotsylvania, had arranged for the seizure of the powder. Residents of Williamsburg were outraged at this action and gathered at the courthouse, which was across from the powder magazine, to demand action. Peyton Randolph, the Speaker of the House of Burgesses and perhaps the most respected politician in Virginia, managed to dissuade the crowd from marching on the Governor's Palace to threaten Dunmore. Randolph met with the governor, instead, to request the return of the powder. Dunmore gave a feeble explanation for his actions and promised to deliver the powder as soon as it was needed, but he refused to return it to the magazine, which he claimed was not secure.

Surprisingly, the large crowd that had gathered at the courthouse to await Dunmore's reply acquiesced to Speaker Randolph's pleas for calm and dispersed without further incident. The same was not true outside of Williamsburg, where the news of Dunmore's actions spread quickly, punctuated by reports of his threat to burn down the capital and to arm his slaves if a mob dared threaten Dunmore or his family again.

Militia March on Williamsburg

News of the gunpowder incident travelled over 100 miles to Fredericksburg in three days. The Spotsylvania County Independent Militia Company happened to be exercising in town when the news arrived on April 24th. The company officers, led by Captain Hugh Mercer, immediately sent dispatches about the incident to the surrounding county militia companies. The dispatches urged the militia companies to assemble in Fredericksburg on April 29th for a march on the capital to retrieve the stolen gunpowder:

Fredericksburgh, Virginia, April 24, 1775.

SIR: From undoubted authority, we received here this...morning, the very disagreeable intelligence, that in the night of Thursday last, Captain Collins, Commander of one of His Majesty' s Sloops of War, by command of his Excellency the Governour, assisted by a Company of Marines, carried off all the Powder from the Magazine in the City of Williamsburgh, and deposited it on board his vessel, which lay at Burwell's Ferry, about five miles below the City.

The said authority informs us that the Corporation of the City of Williamsburgh addressed the Governour on that occasion. The people have received no satisfaction; nor are they likely to recover the Powder, though it is so very necessary for the security of the Country.

This being a day of meeting of the Independent Company of this Town, they considered it necessary to take the matter into serious consideration, and are come to a unanimous resolution, that a submission to so arbitrary an exertion of Government, may not only prejudice the common cause, by introducing a suspicion of a defection of this Colony from the noble pursuit, but will encourage the tools of despotism to commit further acts of violence in this Colony, and more especially subject the Arms in the Magazine to the same fate as the Powder.

In these, sentiments, this Company could but determine that a number of publick spirited gentlemen should embrace this opportunity of showing their zeal in the grand cause, by marching to Williamsburgh to inquire into this affair, and there to take such steps as may best answer the purpose of recovering the Powder, and securing the Arms now in the Magazine.

To this end, they have determined to hold themselves in readiness to march from this place as Light-Horse, on Saturday morning; [April 29th] *and, in the mean time, to submit the matter to the determination of yours and the neighbouring Counties, to whom expresses are purposely forwarded. We address you in the name of our Company, as its Officers, and are, Sir, your very humble servants,*

HUGH MERCER *G. WEEDON*
ALEX SPOTSWOOD *JNO.WILLIS* [27]

Captain Mercer and his fellow officers also wrote directly to Colonel Washington (who was widely viewed as the most militarily qualified Virginian in the colony). Washington had already been honored with the command of several local independent militia companies and now Captain Mercer felt compelled to update him on the actions and intentions of the Spotsylvania County company:

---

[27] Stanislaus Murray Hamilton, ed., "Officers of the Independent Militia Company of Fredericksburg to Captain William Grayson," *Letters to Washington and Accompanying Papers, 1775-1777,* Vol. 1, (Boston and New York: Society of the Colonial Dames of America, 1898), 163-164

Fredericksburgh, April 26, 1775.

SIR: By intelligence from Williamsburgh, it appears that Captain Collins, of His Majesty' s Navy, at the head of fifteen Marines, carried off the Powder from the Magazine in that City on the night of Thursday last, and conveyed it on board his vessel, by order of the Governour.

The gentlemen of the Independent Company of this Town think this first publick insult is not to be tamely submitted to, and determine, with your approbation, to join any other bodies of armed men who are willing to appear in support of the honour of Virginia, as well as to secure the military stores yet remaining in the Magazine.

It is proposed to march from hence on Saturday next for Williamsburgh, properly accoutred as Light-horsemen. Expresses are sent off to inform the Commanding Officers of Companies in the adjacent Counties of this our resolution, and we shall wait prepared for your instructions and their assistance.[28]

It is unclear how Colonel Washington responded to the letter. His diary mentions nothing of it and notes that on the day the militia gathered in Fredericksburg, Washington was, "*home all day.*"[29]

---

[28] Runge, ed., "From Spotsylvania Independent Company, 26 April, 1775," *The Papers of George Washington, Colonial Series,* Vol. 10, 346-347

[29] Donald Jackson, ed., " 29 April, 1775" *The Diaries of George Washington,1771-75,* Vol. 3 (Charlottesville: University Press of Virginia, 1978), 323

Approximately 600 mounted militia answered Mercer's call to assemble in Fredericksburg on April 29th.[30] They were ready to ride to Williamsburg to demand the return of the gunpowder. Many were troubled by news from the north (which arrived a day earlier) of bloodshed between British regulars and colonial militia in the Massachusetts countryside. Despite this unsettling report, the militia that were gathered in Fredericksburg remained focused on the situation in Williamsburg and anxiously waited for the latest news from the capital. It arrived on the evening of April 28th via dispatch riders. The riders brought surprising news, specifically, a request from Peyton Randolph and the other leaders of Williamsburg for the militia in Fredericksburg to cancel their planned march to the capital. Speaker Randolph explained the reason behind his request in a letter to the militia:

> *His Excellency* [Dunmore]...*has given private assurances to Several Gentlemen, that the Powder shall be Return'd to the Magazine.... The Governor considers his Honor as at Stake; he thinks that he acts for the best and will not be compell'd to what we have abundant Reason to believe he would Cheerfully do, were he left to himself* [return the gunpowder]. *It is our opinion and most earnest request that Matters may be quieted for the present at least; we are firmly persuaded that perfect Tranquility will be Speedily Restored; by pursuing this Course we foresee no Hazard of even inconvenience that can ensure,*

---

[30] Robert L. Scribner, ed., "Spotsylvania Council Pledge of Readiness at a Moment's Warning, 29 April, 1775," *Revolutionary Virginia: The Road to Independence,* Vol. 3, (Charlottesville, VA: University Press of Virginia, 1977), 70

> *whereas we are apprehensive...that violent measures may produce effects, which God only knows the consequence of.*[31]

One hundred and two representatives from fourteen militia companies as well as the civilian leadership of Spotsylvania County assembled met to consider whether the planned march to Williamsburg should proceed. After much debate, Captain Mercer and the other representatives agreed to postpone it. They explained their actions in a resolution:

> *Highly condemning the conduct of the Governor on this occasion, as impolitic, and justly alarming to the good people of this colony, tending to destroy all confidence in Government, and to widen the unhappy breach between Great Britain and her colonies...*[but] *at the same time justly dreading the horrors of civil war, influenced by motives of the strongest affection to our fellow subjects of Great Britain, most ardently wishing to heal our mutual wounds and therefore preferring peaceable measures whilst the least hope of reconciliation remains,* [we] *do advise that the several companies now rendezvoused here do return to their respective homes.*[32]

Not everyone was happy with the decision to halt the march from Fredericksburg. Patrick Henry had gathered a

---

[31] Ibid., "Peyton Randolph to Mann Page, Jr., Lewis Willis, and Benjamin Grymes, 27 April, 1775, " 64

[32] Ibid., "Spotsylvania Council Pledge of Readiness at a Moment's Warning, 29 April, 1775," 70-71

force of approximately 150 militia in Hanover County and he proceeded to march to within 16 miles of Williamsburg before he halted.[33] An agreement was eventually struck that temporarily defused the crisis; Lord Dunmore agreed to pay for the seized gunpowder and in return Patrick Henry declared victory and ended his march. Henry then proceeded to join the 2nd Continental Congress in Philadelphia.

Virginia Prepares for War

The situation in Virginia and the rest of the American colonies remained tense into the summer of 1775. The bloodshed continued in Massachusetts when British troops stormed Breed's Hill (known historically as Bunker Hill) in June. The Continental Congress in Philadelphia assumed responsibility for the colonial troops encamped outside of Boston and appointed one of their own delegates, George Washington, to command them. In Virginia, Lord Dunmore created a new crisis by fleeing the capital for the safety of a British warship. There was a real possibility that the bloodshed that occurred in Massachusetts could spread to Virginia, and the colony's political leaders sought to prepare for it by holding another special convention.

The 3rd Virginia Convention met in Richmond, its primary task, to organize Virginia's military forces. With the old militia laws of the colony expired and /or ineffective because of Governor Dunmore's resistance, the Convention adopted an entirely new military system for Virginia. It consisted of three tiers, the first being two regiments of full time soldiers (regulars) raised to serve for a year. The Convention

---

[33] Purdie, *Virginia Gazette Supplement,* 5 May, 1775, 2

organized Virginia into sixteen districts and ordered each district to recruit and send a company (sixty-eight men) of regular troops to Williamsburg for the two regiments as soon as possible.[34]

The regular troops were not the only soldiers to be raised. The second tier of Virginia's new military establishment comprised sixteen battalions of minutemen. These men were drawn from the ranks of the militia and were "*more strictly trained to proper discipline*" than the ordinary militia. Each district was ordered to raise a 500 man battalion of minutemen "*from the age of sixteen to fifty, to be divided into ten companies of fifty men each.*"[35] Once the minute battalions raised the necessary men, they were to muster and train for twenty straight days. Following this, the companies of each minute battalion were expected to exercise on their own for four days every month. Additionally, after the twenty day drill, each battalion was to assemble for twelve day training sessions twice a year.[36]

The last tier of Virginia's new military establishment was the traditional county militia. The Convention decreed that:

> *All male persons, hired servants, and apprentices, above the age of sixteen, and under fifty years...shall be enlisted into the militia...and formed into companies.*[37]

Each member of the county militia had six months to furnish himself with

---

[34] William W. Hening, *The Statutes at Large Being a Collection of all the Laws of Virginia*, Vol. 9, (Richmond: J. & G. Cochran, 1821), 10, 16

[35] Ibid., 16-17

[36] Ibid., 20

[37] Ibid., 27-28

> *A good rifle...with a tomahawk,* [or a] *common firelock, bayonet, pouch, or cartouch box, three charges of powder and ball....* [Members of the militia] *shall constantly keep by him one pound of powder and four pounds of ball....*[38]

The militia companies were ordered to hold private musters every two weeks, except in December, January, and February.

Mercer Considered for Command

The Convention turned its attention to the command of the two regular regiments in early August. Patrick Henry, the most popular political leader in Virginia, attracted the support of a number of delegates, but his lack of military experience, coupled with a strong dislike of the man by a number of delegates, put his selection in doubt. Opponents of Henry hoped that Thomas Nelson Jr. would challenge Henry, but Nelson begged off due to health concerns, so Henry's opponents turned to Hugh Mercer.[39]

Dr. Mercer's extensive military experience in the French and Indian War made him an excellent choice to command Virginia 1st Regiment of regulars, and after the first ballot, the Scotsman held a one vote lead over Henry, 41 to 40.[40] Thomas Nelson Jr. and William Woodford attracted nine votes between them and it fell to these nine votes to determine the election. A second ballot was held between the two leading

---

[38] Ibid.

[39] Scribner, ed., "Endnote 6," *Revolutionary Virginia: The Road to Independence,* Vol. 3, 402

[40] Ibid., "Proceedings of the Fifteenth Day of the Third Virginia Convention, 5 August, 1775," 400

candidates and six of the nine votes up for grabs swung to Henry, which put him over the top.[41]

One account of the debate and vote noted that

> *Mr. Mercer was objected to for being a North Briton. In answer to this objection, it was admitted that Mr. Mercer was born in Scotland, but that he came to America in his early years, and had constantly resided in it from his first coming over, that his family, and all his other connections, were in this colony, that he had uniformly distinguished himself a warm and firm friend to the rights of America, and what was of principal consideration that he was possessed great military as well as literary abilities.*[42]

Unfortunately for Dr. Mercer, the bias against his Scottish background apparently carried over into the selection of the 2nd Virginia Regiment's commander. William Woodford of Caroline County (an acquaintance of Mercer's and fellow veteran of the French and Indian War) was selected by the convention to command the 2nd Virginia Regiment.

Mercer Commands a Minute Battalion

Dr. Mercer's neighbors and friends rallied to Mercer's support just a month later when it was time to appoint the commander of the minute battalion for the counties of Spotsylvania, Caroline, King George, and Stafford County. Although Spotsylvania representatives on the committee made

---

[41] Ibid., "Endnote 7," 403

[42] Purdie, *Virginia Gazette*, 9 February, 1776, 3

up only a portion of the Caroline District Committee, they led the fight for Mercer's appointment, and he was named Colonel of the Caroline District Minute Battalion on September 12, 1775.[43]

The Spotsylvania County committee expressed its approval of Mercer's appointment in a resolution in September:

> *The committee of the county, to express their approbation of the appointment of col. Mercer, and to pay a tribute justly due to the noble and patriotick conduct which that gentleman has uniformly pursued since the commencement of our disputes with the mother country, which was so strikingly displayed on that occasion, entered into the following resolve:*
>
> *Resolved unanimously, that the thanks of this committee be presented to col. HUGH MERCER, commander in chief of the battalion of minute men in the district of this county, the counties of Caroline, Stafford, and King George, expressing our high sense of the importance of the county of his appointment to that station, and our acknowledgments of his publick spirit in sacrificing his private interest to the service of his country.*[44]

Mercer's leadership was acknowledged again by his fellow freeholders two months later when he was elected to serve on

---

[43] Robert L. Scribner and Brent Tarter, eds., "Caroline District Committee: Election of Officers of Regulars and of Minutemen, 12 September 1775," *Revolutionary Virginia: The Road to Independence,* Vol. 4 (Charlottesville, VA: University Press of Virginia, 1978), 99

[44] Ibid., "Spotsylvania County Committee: An Approbation and a Tribute Justly Due, September 1775," 103-104

a new county committee charged with, "*carrying into execution the association, and such other measures as the continental congress, or general convention of this colony, have* [passed]…."[45] In other words, this new committee was to enforce the provisions of both Congress and the Virginia Conventions within Spotsylvania County.

Colonel Mercer's military duties prevented his active participation on this committee. In early November, Mercer's minute battalion camped on William Daingerfield's plantation, Belvidera, about seven miles south of Fredericksburg to begin twenty days of training.[46] John Harrower, the tutor of Mr. Daingerfield's children, described the arrival of the minutemen in his diary:

> *Upon Thursday 2d Inst. there was a Camp Marked out close at the back of the school for a Battalion of 500 private men besides officers and they immediately began to erect tents for the same.* [On November 9th] *the whole was finished for 250 men being 50 tents for the privates & 6 ditto for officers & 3 ditto for the Comissary & his Stores…. This day the 250 men being 5 Companys from different parts arrived at the Camp the other 5 Companys not being as yet completed.*[47]

For the next three weeks, the minute-men under Colonel Mercer exercised and drilled at Belvidera. Harrower noted one mishap three days into the encampment when an officer's

---

[45] Ibid., "Spotsylvania County Committee, 16 November, 1775," 417 and Hening, *The Statutes at Large Being a Collection of all the Laws of Virginia*, Vol. 9, 57

[46] Riley, ed., "9 November 1775," *The Journal of John Harrower: An Indentured Servant in the Colony of Virginia, 1773-1776*, 124

[47] Ibid., "9 November, 1775," 124

tent caught on fire, but no one was injured and nothing of any value was lost except the tent.[48] At the end of the month the troops were dismissed to their homes.[49] Like everyone else in Virginia, they turned their attention to southeastern Virginia, where Lord Dunmore appeared to make significant gains in his effort to re-establish royal control over the colony.

War in Virginia

Although much blood had been shed in Massachusetts during the spring and summer of 1775, six months passed in Virginia before the first shots were fired between Governor Dunmore's forces and those he deemed rebels. It began in Hampton, where two days of fighting erupted in late October between a small naval squadron led by Captain Mathew Squire of the *H.M.S. Otter* (who was determined to burn Hampton) and Virginia ground troops from the 2nd Virginia Regiment, the Culpeper Minute Battalion, and the local militia. The rebel forces succeeded in stopping the ships and Hampton was spared, but Lord Dunmore remained on the offensive, skirmishing with rebel troops near Jamestown Island and in Princess Anne and Norfolk Counties. Dunmore's forces routed a militia force at Kemp's Landing in Princess Anne County in mid-November, prompting the governor to raise the King's standard and issue a proclamation requiring all loyal Virginians to come to his aid. The proclamation also offered freedom to any runaway slave or indentured servant of a rebel who agreed to fight for Lord Dunmore:

---

[48] Ibid., "12 November, 1775," 125
[49] Ibid., "29 November, 1775," 127

> *I do in Virtue of the Power and Authority to ME given, by His Majesty, determine to execute Martial Law, and cause the same to be executed throughout this Colony: and to the end that Peace and good Order may the sooner be restored, I do require every Person capable of bearing Arms, to resort to His Majesty's STANDARD, or be looked upon as Traitors to His Majesty's Crown and Government, and thereby become liable to the Penalty the Law inflicts upon such Offences; such as forfeiture of Life, confiscation of Lands, &c. &c And I do hereby further declare all indentured Servants, Negroes, or others (appertaining to Rebels,) free that are able and willing to bear Arms, they joining His Majesty's Troops as soon as may be, for the more speedily reducing this Colony to a proper Sense of their Duty, to His Majesty's Crown and Dignity....*[50]

Lord Dunmore was very pleased with the response to his proclamation, reporting to General Howe in Boston that

> *Immediately on* [the victory at Kemp's Landing] *I issued the inclosed Proclamation which has had a Wonderful effect as there are not less than three thousand that have already taken and signed the inclosed Oath.*[51]

Dunmore added that

---

[50] William Clark, ed., "Lord Dunmore's Proclamation," *Naval Documents of the American Revolution,* Vol. 2, (Washington, DC: U.S . Government Printing Office, 1966), 920

[51] Clark, ed., "Lord Dunmore to General William Howe, 30 November, 1775," *Naval Documents of the American Revolution*, Vol. 2, 1209-11

> *The Negroes are flocking in also from all quarters which I hope will oblige the Rebels to disperse to take care of their families, and property, and had I but a few more men here I would March immediately to Williamsburg my former place of residence by which I should soon compel the whole Colony to Submit.*[52]

With only 120 British regulars from the 14th Regiment of Foot with him as the backbone of his force, Dunmore was not ready to march on Williamsburg. He was however, ready to secure Norfolk as a base of operation, and one of the keys to securing Norfolk was holding the Great Bridge, 11 miles south of Norfolk.

Great Bridge

Reports of a large rebel force on its way to Norfolk prompted Dunmore to dig in and secure a key river crossing at the Great Bridge in late November. He explained his actions to General Howe:

> *Having heard that a thousand chosen Men belonging to the Rebels, a great part of which were Rifle men, were on their March to attack us here so to cut off our provisions, I determined to take possession of the pass at the great Bridge which Secures us the greatest part of two Counties to supply us with provisions. I accordingly ordered a Stockade Fort to be erected there, which was done in a few days, and I put an Officer and Twenty five men to Garrison it,*

52 Ibid.

with some Volunteers and Negroes, who have defended it against all efforts of the Rebels for these eight days past, we have killed Several of their Men, and I make no doubt we shall now be able to maintain our ground there, but should we be obliged to abandon it, we have thrown up an Entrenchment on the Land side of Norfolk which I hope they never will be able to force.[53]

The 'chosen men" opposing Dunmore at Great Bridge were elements of the Culpeper Minute Battalion and six companies of the 2nd Virginia Regiment. Colonel William Woodford commanded the combined force and spent the early part of December probing Dunmore's defenses. Lord Dunmore described some of these probes in a letter to London:

The Fort has been besieged by between seven or eight hundred of the Rebels for these eight days past, without hitherto doing us the least damage, except wounding one or two Men very Slightly…the Rebels…have made many attempts to Cross the [river] *on Rafts, but thank God we have hitherto always repulsed them.*[54]

With both sides entrenched along opposite sides of the river and the bridge dismantled, the stalemate entered a second week. The situation drastically changed on December 9th, when Lord Dunmore's troops suddenly attacked. Colonel Woodford described how a servant of one of his officers

---

[53] Ibid.

[54] Clark, "Dunmore to Lord Dartmouth, 6 December, 1775," *Naval Documents of the American Revolution,* Vol. 2, 1311

provided Dunmore with false information that caused the Governor to stage an ill advised attack:

> *A servant belonging to major* [Thomas] *Marshal, who deserted the other night from col. Charles Scott's party, has completely taken his lordship in. Lieutenant Batut,* [of Britain's 14th Regiment], *who is wounded, and at present my prisoner, informs, that this fellow told them not more than 300 shirtmen were here; and that* [Dunmore took] *the bait, dispatching capt. Leslie with all the regulars (about 200) who arrived at the bridge about 3 o"clock in the morning, joined* [by] *about 300 black and white slaves, laid planks upon the bridge, and crossed just after our reveille had beat…capt. Fordyce of the grenadiers led the* [attack] *with his company, who, for coolness and bravery, deserved a better fate, as well as the brave fellows who fell with him, who behaved like heroes. They marched up to our breastwork with fixed bayonets, and perhaps a hotter fire never happened, or a greater carnage, for the number of troops.*[55]

A similar account of the attack was given by a British midshipman:

> *We marched up to their works with the intrepidity of lions. But, alas! We retreated with much fewer brave fellows than we took out. Their fire was so heavy, that, had we not retreated as we did, we should every one have*

---

[55] Clark, "Colonel William Woodford to Edmund Pendleton, 10 December, 1775," *Naval Documents of the American Revolution,* Vol. 3, 39-40

> *been cut off. Figure to yourself a strong breast-work built across a causeway, on which six men only could advance a-breast; a large swamp almost surrounding them, at the back of which were two small breast-works to flank us in our attack on their intrenchments. Under these disadvantages it was impossible to succeed; yet our men were so enraged, that all the intreaties, and...threats of their Officers could* [not convince] *them to retreat; which at last they did...We had sixty killed, wounded, and taken prisoner....*[56]

The Virginians were thrilled with their victory. Nineteen year old John Marshall, a lieutenant in the Culpeper Minutemen and a future Chief Justice of the Supreme Court, noted that

> *Every grenadier is said to have been killed or wounded in this ill-judged attack, while the Americans did not lose a single man.*[57]

Colonel Woodford's report was equally upbeat. He declared that the battle "*was a second Bunker's Hill affair, in miniature, with this difference, that we kept our post.*"[58]

The "rebel" victory at Great Bridge forced Lord Dunmore to abandon Norfolk and withdraw to the safety of British ships anchored in the Elizabeth River. Although this was a serious

---

[56] Clark, "Letter from a Midshipman on Board H.M. Sloop Otter, 9 December, 1775," *Naval Documents of the American Revolution,* Vol. 3, 29

[57] John Marshall, *The Life of George Washington, Vol. 2*, (Fredericksburg, VA: The Citizens Guild of Washington's Boyhood Home, 1926), 132

[58] Clark, "Colonel William Woodford to Edmund Pendleton, 10 December, 1775," *Naval Documents of the American Revolution,* Vol. 3, 40

setback for Dunmore's efforts to re-establish royal authority in Virginia, his chastised force remained a military threat, one that the 4th Virginia Convention addressed just days after the Battle of Great Bridge.

Chapter Three

"Colonel Mercer Has Done Great Things Towards a Reform...."

December 1775 – June 1776

Declaring that they must, "*repel force with force*," the delegates of Virginia's 4th Convention, meeting in Williamsburg on December 13th, 1775, voted to raise six additional regiments of regular troops to reinforce the two that already existed.[1] Colonel Hugh Mercer was the overwhelming choice of the convention to command the first of the new regiments, the 3rd Virginia Regiment.[2] Mercer's brother-in-law, George Weedon, joined Colonel Mercer as the regiment's Lieutenant-Colonel and Thomas Marshall of Fauquier County (the father of future Supreme Court Chief Justice John Marshall) was appointed Major of the regiment.[3]

It was the responsibility of the company grade officers (captains and lieutenants) of each regiment to recruit the soldiers. The 3rd Virginia, like all of the new regiments of regulars, consisted of ten companies of 68 rank and file each.

---

1 Robert L. Scribner and Brent Tarter, eds., "Proceedings of the 4th Virginia Convention, 13 December, 1775," *Revolutionary Virginia: The Road to Independence,* Vol. 5 (Charlottesville, VA: University Press of Virginia, 1979), 128

2 Ibid., "Proceedings of the 4th Virginia Convention, 11 January, 1776," 383

3 Ibid., "Proceedings of the 4th Virginia Convention, 12 January, 1776," 391-392

The Virginia Convention determined the number of companies each county was to raise and which regiment they were assigned to. The bulk of the companies assigned to the 3rd Virginia came from counties in the northern region of Virginia, specifically, Fairfax, Loudoun, Prince William (2), Stafford, Fauquier, Culpeper, King George, Louisa, and Spotsylvania counties. Company officers appointed by committees from these counties worked hard over the winter to recruit. While they did so, news arrived in February that the Continental Congress had put the six new regiments upon the Continental establishment. This meant that Congress assumed authority over them.[4]

Colonel Mercer and Lieutenant-Colonel Weedon travelled to Williamsburg in early March and received their commissions. Mercer found the troops of the 1st Virginia Regiment, posted at Williamsburg, in some disarray, due in part to the recent resignation of Colonel Patrick Henry. Colonel Henry, angry at being passed over for promotion by the Continental Congress, had resigned his commission as commander of the 1st Virginia in late February. The news of Henry's resignation prompted a near mutiny in the ranks of his old regiment; the troops went into, "*deep mourning*" and many demanded their discharge in response to Henry's departure.[5] Luckily, Colonel Henry was able to calm the situation, but it was a surly group of disgruntled soldiers that were encamped in Williamsburg when Colonel Mercer arrived, and as the ranking officer in town, he temporarily assumed command over them..

---

[4] Ibid., "Continental Congress, 13 February, 1776," 89

[5] Purdie, *Virginia Gazette*, 1 March, 1776, 3

Colonel Mercer immediately recognized the need for greater discipline among the troops, both rank and file and officers, and issued orders accordingly. He declared in general orders that officers were answerable for any disturbance of the peace in town caused by their men and instructed company officers to frequently inspect the quarters of the troops for damage and cleanliness.[6] Officers were also instructed to exercise their men more to enhance discipline, yet, "*Treat the Soldiers With the utmost Humanity and Tenderness....*" [7] Mercer reminded the troops themselves that

> *Every Soldier is to Consider himself as intended to Protect the inhabitants of this Country* [so] *if contrary to this intention* [a soldier] *should insult or injure* [the inhabitants] *in their persons or property, he may Depend on being Treated with Severity.*[8]

Edmund Pendleton, president of the Committee of Safety, acknowledged Mercer's progress with the troops but also noted some resistance to his efforts:

> *Colonel Mercer has done great things towards a Reform which has given great pleasure to the Judicious, but I understand has produced a Court of Enquiry into his Conduct....*[9]

---

[6] R. A. Brock, ed., "General Orders, 5 and 7 March, in The Orderly Book of the Company of Captain George Stubblefield, Fifth Virginia Regiment, from March 3 to July 10, 1776, " *Collections of the Virginia Historical Society*, New Series, Vol. 6, (Richmond, VA: 1888), 145-147

[7] Ibid., General Orders 7 and 11 March, 1776," 147, 149-150

[8] Ibid., "General Orders, 7 March, 1776," 147

[9] David John Mays, ed., "To William Woodford, 16 March, 1776," *The Letters and Papers of Edmund Pendleton, 1734-1803,* Vol. 1, (Charlottesville, VA: University Press of Virginia, 1967,) 158-159

Mutiny of Gibson's Lambs

The specific incident that sparked an inquiry into Mercer's conduct involved Captain George Gibson's company of Augusta County riflemen (who were under Lieutenant William Lynn's command in Gibson's absence). These frontiersmen, known sarcastically as Gibson's lambs, bristled at Mercer's efforts to reign in their behavior, and when two of them were lightly punished by a court martial for behavior that Colonel Mercer believed was "*seditious*", he disapproved of the sentence and had the men placed in irons until Brigadier-General Robert Howe arrived to take up the matter.[10] If that had been all Mercer did, the matter might have ended there, but Colonel Mercer was determined to end the rampant defiance to military authority in Gibson's company and took the additional step of disarming the rest of Gibson's riflemen and placed them, under guard, upon fatigue duty. He explained his action in the after orders of March 11th:

> *In Consequence of the seditious behavior of some of Capt. Gibson's Comp'y, two of them were Confin'd and a General Court Martial of the Line instituted, the Sentence of which the Commanding Officer Totally Disapproved. It is ordered that the Two Prisoners be Laid in Irons...till the arrival of Genl. Howe. The Rest of the Comp'y, non-com'd officers and Rank and File, having* [displayed] *on* [many] *occasions the Same Seditious and Mutinous Spirit, Shall be Stript of their arms and ammunition, and Put upon Duty of Fatigue under the Direction of the Quarter-Master Genl, who*

---

[10] Brock, ed., "After Orders, 11 March, 1776, " 150-151

> *shall be Supported in the Execution of his Duty by a Captain's Guard, Properly Furnish'd with ammunition. The Captain of that Guard is to have orders, that if any of these Seditious and Mutinous Soldiers Shall dare to Refuse to Perform the Duty which the Quarter-Master Shall direct, such offenders shall be put in Irons…*[and] *if any obstruction arise from the same Mutinous Disposition, the Guard is to fire on the offenders With such Effect as to kill them if possible.*[11]

Mercer's harsh directive was successful in containing Captain Gibson's company, but his threat to shoot any offender of his orders was challenged by the officers of Gibson's company as too extreme, and they appealed to General Howe when he arrived in Williamsburg in mid-March. The result was an apology from Colonel Mercer posted in the general orders of March 17th:

> *Head-Quarters, March 17, 1776*
> *General Orders -- Col. Mercer, sensible that he exceeded the line of duty in his treatment of capt. Gibson's company, has requested the commanding-officer to declare, in orders, that he had no personal intention in any thing he did, and in this publick manner desires to acknowledge he was wrong, and assures the company he is sorry for what happened. The commanding officer is of opinion, that this officer-like acknowledgement of the colonel's ought to be satisfactory to the company.*[12]

---

[11] Ibid., "After Orders 11 March, 1776," 150-151
[12] Purdie, *Virginia Gazette*, 5 April, 1776," 3

Lieutenant Lynn of Gibson's company, responding to negative reports and rumors about the conduct of his company, sent a copy of Mercer's comments to the gazettes, which published it in early April.[13] An angry Colonel Mercer, who had returned to northern Virginia to command the 3rd Virginia, replied to Lynn with his own letter to the gazettes.

> *Fredericksburg, April 10, 1776*
> *The publick, to whom lient. Lynn thought proper to report an affair of military discipline, will naturally conclude from his publication that I have injured the characters of the men of capt. Gibson's company of regulars. I aimed at mending the character of that company, and hope I have not missed my aim. In attempting this necessary service, it is true, some deviation was made from the line of duty; but whose deviation from duty was most injurious to that company, and to the cause in which we are engaged, I beg leave also to submit to the publick: That of an officer who quells a mutinous spirit in the troops, or of those officers who, by a neglect of discipline, had, after some months training, obliged me to take the trouble of reducing their men to some degree of military order.*[14]

Colonel Mercer asserted that his actions towards Gibson's company were for the good of both Gibson's men (who lacked sufficient discipline) and the army in general. He also placed the blame for the incident upon Lieutenant Lynn and his

---

[13] Ibid.
[14] Purdie, *Virginia Gazette*, 19 April, 1776," 4

fellow officers who, Mercer contended, had neglected to adequately discipline their troops in the months leading up to the incident and had thus helped create the mutinous spirit of the men.

Guarding the Potomac

Colonel Mercer's response to Lynn was written in Fredericksburg on April 10th. Two weeks earlier, Mercer had rejoined his regiment at Dumfries, the muster station for the 3rd Virginia. The Virginia Convention had given Colonel Mercer and his regiment the responsibility of guarding the upper portion of the Potomac River. The lower half of the river was guarded by the 5th Virginia Regiment commanded by Colonel William Peachy. A month earlier in March, Colonel Mercer and Colonel Peachy were instructed by the Virginia Convention to work with authorities in Maryland to erect a chain of beacons from the mouth of the Potomac all the way to Alexandria (approximately 100 miles) to warn of the approach of the enemy.[15]

Colonel Mercer was also very busy organizing his regiment, which slowly gathered in Dumfries in March and April.[16] Only five companies were present in Dumfries in early April, three other companies had been detached to Hampton in southeast Virginia, and two others had yet to arrive in Dumfries. Despite the missing companies, Mercer

---

[15] Robert L. Scribner and Brent Tarter, eds., "Proceeding of the Virginia Committee of Safety, 6 March, 1776," *Revolutionary Virginia: The Road to Independence,* Vol. 6 (Charlottesville, VA: University Press of Virginia, 1981), 175

[16] Philander D. Chase, ed., "Lund Washington to George Washington, 29 February, 1776, *The Papers of George Washington,* Vol. 3, (Charlottesville, VA: University Press of Virginia, 1988), 396

was short on tents and waited impatiently for some to arrive. Once they did, Mercer planned to leave a detachment of troops in Dumfries and march the rest of his regiment to Alexandria to, "*encamp…for the purpose of training the Officers and men.*"[17]

The presence of the 3rd Virginia Regiment gave some comfort to George Mason in Fairfax County. He wrote to his friend, General Washington on April 2nd that,

> *A regiment commanded by Colonel Mercer of Fredericksburg, is stationed on this part of the river, and I hope we shall be tolerably safe, unless a push is made here with a large body of men.*[18]

Mason would undoubtedly have been troubled to learn that on the same day he wrote to Washington, orders were sent to Colonel Mercer to march the 3rd Virginia to Williamsburg. The orders came from newly arrived General Charles Lee. General Lee, who was not a Virginian or even a colonist, but rather, a recently arrived Englishman with significant experience in the British army, had been sent to the South by the Continental Congress to lead the defense of the southern colonies against an expected British attack. Lee had spent the previous year with General Washington outside of Boston and was widely viewed and admired as the most competent of all of the officers in the continental army.

---

[17] "Col. Hugh Mercer to Gen. Lee, 1 April, 1776", *The Lee Papers*, Vol. 1, (Collections of the New York Historical Society, 1871), 371

[18] Kate Mason Rowland, "George Mason to George Washington, 2 April, 1776," *The Life and Correspondence of George Mason,* Vol. 1, (New York: Russell & Russell, 1964), 219

When General Lee arrived in Williamsburg in late March and assumed command of Virginia's forces he immediately set out to replace the Convention's regional defense plan (which scattered Virginia's eight regiments throughout Virginia) with a new arrangement that concentrated the troops around Williamsburg. A concentration of forces, argued Lee, allowed for offensive action against Lord Dunmore (who remained near Portsmouth in the Elizabeth River) as well as stronger defensive capabilities should the enemy suddenly strike Virginia.[19]

On April 2nd, General Lee ordered Colonel Mercer to march his regiment to Williamsburg as quickly as possible:

> *As there is the greatest reason to conclude…that if the enemy arrive with a considerable force, the possession of Williamsburg and York will be their first object…I think it necessary…to defeat…their design. I must therefore desire that you will march your Regiment to* [Williamsburg] *without delay.*[20]

It took a few days for Lee's order to reach Mercer and then a few more for the colonel to organize his regiment for the march. Poor weather also delayed Mercer's march south. On April 10th, he wrote to General Lee from Fredericksburg:

> *In obedience to your orders…my Regiment is on the march from Alexandria & Dumfries, we are much retarded by daily succeeding Rains, which have*

---

[19] Scribner and Tarter, eds., "An Introductory Note," *Revolutionary Virginia: The Road to Independence,* Vol. 6, 277

[20] "General Charles Lee to Colonel Hugh Mercer, 2 April, 1776," *The Lee Papers,* Vol. 1, 369

> *render'd the Roads almost impassable, but will use our utmost endeavour to be soon at Williamsburg.*[21]

The delay was fortunate because at the prompting of the Committee of Safety, General Lee reversed his decision. He ordered Colonel Mercer to remain in northern Virginia and deploy his regiment as he thought best to defend the region:

> *I must desire that you will remain with your Regiment for the defence of* [northern Virginia and] *as you are a much better judge of the manner to station them, than I can possibly be; for instance, whether the whole or only a part* [should be posted] *at Alexandria, I leave* [it] *entirely to your good sense and discretion.*[22]

Colonel Mercer replied to Lee's order on April 14th:

> *I shall prepare in obedience to your orders…to resume my former station at Alexandria. That place…*[has] *a considerable quantity of public stores, & appears to me to be the principle object, we are to attend to in defence of the frontier along the Potowmack River. Guards will also be necessary on* [Occoquan], *Quantico, & Patowmack Creeks. I should judge that my Regiment cannot occupy further along that Frontier without dividing us too much.*[23]

---

[21] Ibid., " Colonel Hugh Mercer to Gen. Charles Lee, 10 April, 1776, 406

[22] Ibid., "General Charles Lee to Colonel Hugh Mercer, 10 April, 1776, 409

[23] Ibid., "Colonel Hugh Mercer to Gen. Charles Lee, 14 April, 1776" 419

Gwynn's Island

Mercer remained in Fredericksburg a few more days, no doubt thankful at the opportunity to see his children and pregnant wife. It was not until late May that the 3rd Virginia was again ordered south to Williamsburg. Lord Dunmore had surprised Virginia's leaders by abandoning his post near Portsmouth and establishing a new base of operation in the Chesapeake Bay on Gwynn's Island. Troops from the 7th Virginia Regiment and the local militia rushed to confront Dunmore, while those further away, like Colonel Mercer and the 3rd Virginia, were ordered to march to Williamsburg.

General Lee had moved on to Charleston, South Carolina in May (where he would help turn back a British invasion force the following month) so the new commander of the forces in Virginia was Brigadier-General Andrew Lewis, an experienced commander from Lord Dunmore's 1774 expedition against the Shawnee. Lewis informed General Lee in a letter on May 27th that Colonel Mercer and his regiment would depart Fredericksburg that day for Williamsburg. [24]

Colonel Mercer and his troops spent about two weeks in Williamsburg in early June before Mercer was ordered to lead three companies to Gwynn's Island to reinforce the 7th Virginia. Mercer's stay at Gwynn's Island was brief, however, for a dispatch from Philadelphia arrived in the capital soon after Mercer reached Gwynn's Island with important news.

---

[24] Ibid., "General Andrew Lewis to General Charles Lee, 27 May, 1776," *The Lee Papers*, Vol. 2, (Collections of the New York Historical Society, 1871), 43

Virginia

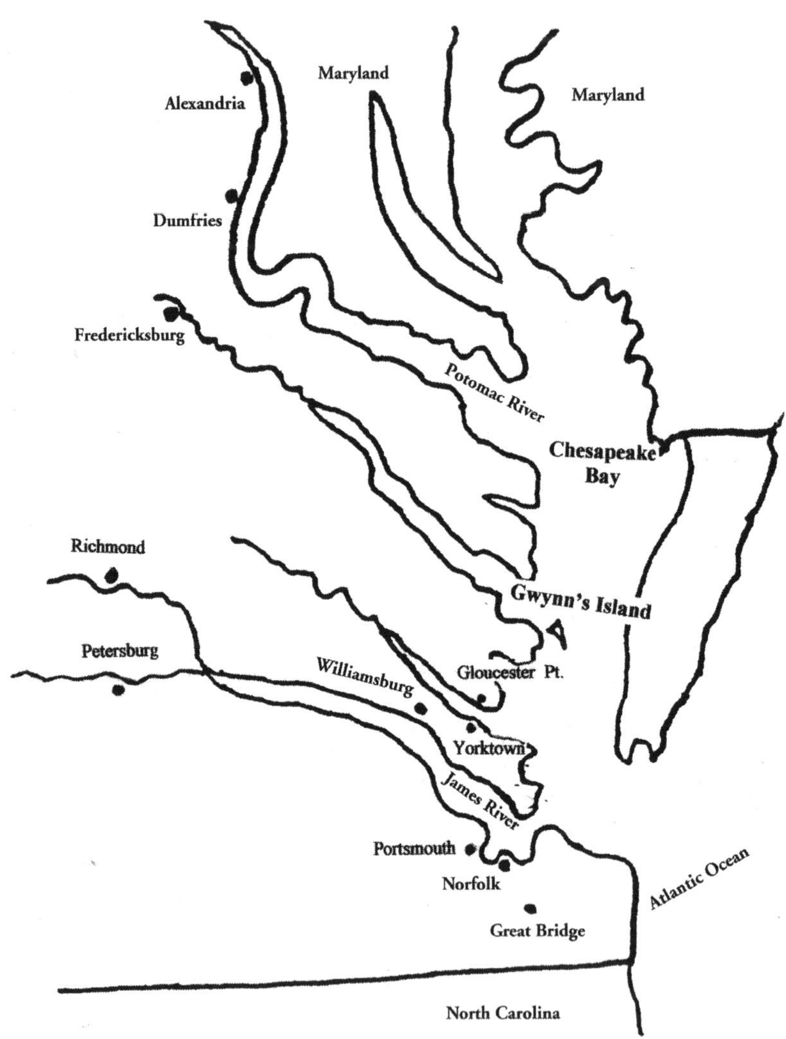
Maryland
Maryland
Alexandria
Dumfries
Fredericksburg
Potomac River
Chesapeake Bay
Richmond
Gwynn's Island
Petersburg
Williamsburg
Gloucester Pt.
Yorktown
James River
Portsmouth
Norfolk
Atlantic Ocean
Great Bridge
North Carolina

Chapter Four

"General Mercer's...Judgment and Experience May be Depended Upon."

June – November 1776

Just days after his arrival at Gwynn's Island in mid-June, Colonel Mercer received a letter from the President of the Continental Congress, John Hancock, informing him that he had been promoted by Congress to the rank of brigadier-general in the continental army.[1] General Mercer immediately returned to Williamsburg where he penned a reply on June 15th.

> *Give me leave, sir, to request of you to present to the honourable Congress my most grateful acknowledgement for this distinguished mark of their regard. I was on duty with part of my regiment before Gwinn's Island, where Lord Dunmore has taken possession, when your instructions reached me; in consequence of those, I shall use my utmost diligence, after settling the accounts of my regiment, to wait on you in Philadelphia.*[2]

---

[1] Worthington C. Ford, ed., "5 June, 1776," *Journal of the Continental Congress,* 1774-1789, Vol. 5 (Washington, D.C., 1906), 420

[2] Peter Force, ed., "Mercer to Congress 15 June, 1776," *American Archives*, Fourth Series, Vol. 6 903

It is probable that on his way north, Mercer stopped in Fredericksburg for one last visit with his wife, Isabella and their children. If he did so, his visit was brief, for he arrived in New York on July 2nd, and reported to General Washington.[3] Mercer was likely greeted warmly by the American commander-in-chief. Washington's absence from Virginia had entered its second year, so he undoubtedly welcomed the chance to visit with a fellow Virginian. General Mercer brought the latest news from home and, in all likelihood, messages from Washington's mother, sister, and friends in Fredericksburg. More importantly (observed Washington to General William Livingston of New Jersey) General Mercer was a commander whose, "*experience & judgment you may repose great confidence*."[4]

General Washington immediately sent Mercer across the Hudson River to Powles Hook to organize the militia and prevent a possible British landing in New Jersey. Such an occurrence was a real concern for Washington because General William Howe's enormous invasion force had finally arrived and landed on Staten Island. The bulk of Washington's army, estimated at 20,000 troops, was stationed in New York (the southern tip of Manhattan Island) and on Long Island (at Brooklyn Heights). Neither force was able to strike Staten Island or adequately defend New Jersey if General Howe suddenly landed troops there.

---

[3] Philander D. Chase, ed., "General Washington to John Hancock, 4-5 July, 1776," *The Papers of George Washington*, Vol. 5, (Charlottesville, VA: University Press of Virginia, 1993), 202

[4] Ibid., "General Washington to Brigadier General William Livingston, 6 July, 1776," 224

General Mercer Commands the Flying Camp

A month earlier, in the beginning of June, the Continental Congress had authorized the formation of a Flying Camp or ready reserve of 10,000 militia comprised of troops from Pennsylvania, Maryland and Delaware.[5] Its purpose was to both defend New Jersey from attack and assist General Washington in the defense of New York, but the Flying Camp troops had not arrived yet so the security of New Jersey rested mainly on the local militia. It was these troops that General Mercer took charge of on July 3rd.

General Mercer's first move was to secure the ferry crossings between New Jersey and Staten Island and relieve the apprehensions of the inhabitants of Newark by stationing troops there.[6] After another meeting with General Washington on July 6th, General Mercer rode to Elizabethtown to confer with General Livingston, the ranking militia commander in New Jersey. Mercer examined Bergen Neck (a peninsula that lay just north of Staten Island) and ordered the removal of a number of cattle and horses to prevent their seizure by the enemy. The 350 militia on Bergen Neck were eager to return to their homes (a sentiment Mercer heard throughout the summer) so he informed General Washington that he intended to replace them with Pennsylvania militia that were reportedly on the march.[7]

---

[5] Worthington C. Ford, ed., "3 June, 1776," *Journal of the Continental Congress, 1774-1789*, Vol. 4, (Washington, D.C., 1906), 412

[6] Chase, ed., "General Washington to Brigadier General Hugh Mercer, 4 July, 1776," *The Papers of George Washington,* Vol. 5, 206

[7] Ibid., "Brigadier General Mercer to General Washington,8 July, 1776," 243

New Jersey and New York

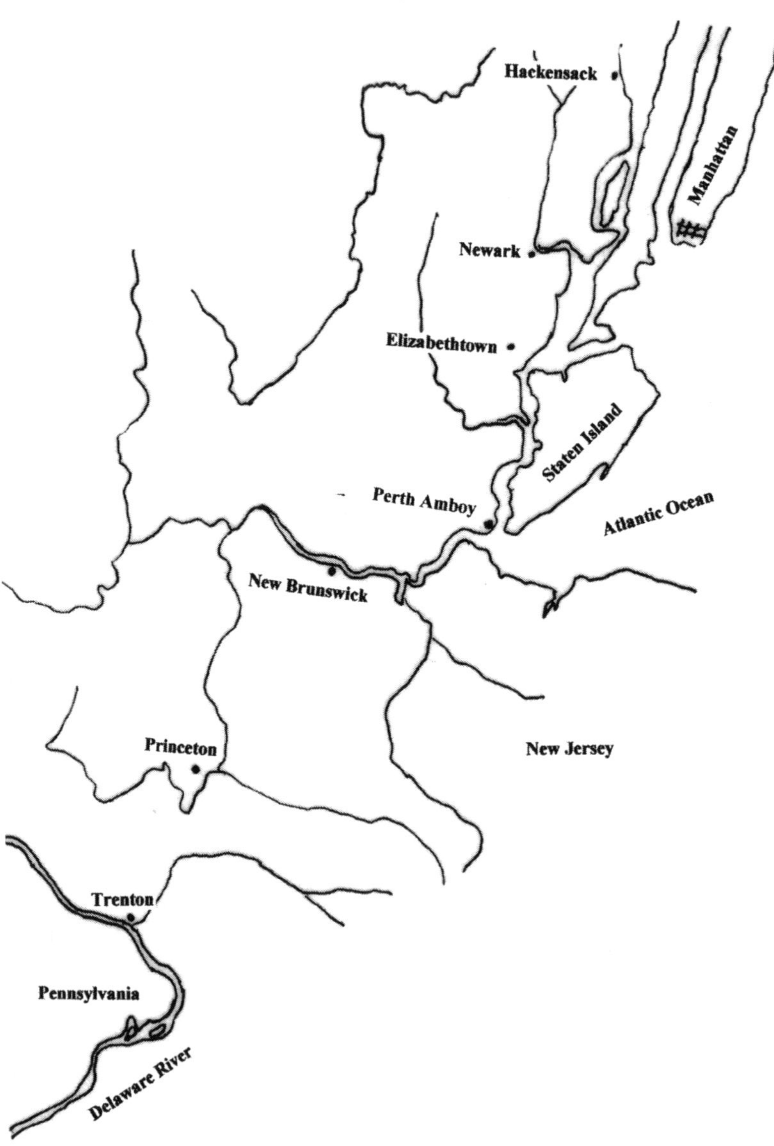

By July 9th, General Mercer was at Perth Amboy, near the mouth of the Raritan River and the southern end of Staten Island, where he assumed command of 1,000 New Jersey militia. These troops, like the militia at Bergen, were also eager to return home. Mercer offered them a compromise and informed General Washington of it:

> [The militia] *begin to be so anxious to return to their Harvest, under the apprehension of their familys being without support...that I have permitted a Draft from each Company to be discharged – about 200 in all – and have assured the others they shall be relieved when the Pennsyla Militia arrive.*[8]

Mercer added that the enemy on Staten Island showed no intention of attacking New Jersey and in fact, had only erected a lone earthwork with two field cannon across the narrow tidal strait (the Arthur Kill) from Perth Amboy.[9] Enemy activity on the western side of Staten Island was so light that General Mercer boldly suggested an attack upon the British.

> *The present situation of the Enemy....rather points out an attempt on their Quarters, which being made at once at different places would probably succeed.*[10]

General Washington proposed just such an attack to a council of war in New York on July 12th, but it was unanimously rejected as too dangerous. Instead, General Mercer, who was absent from the war council, was instructed

---

[8] Ibid., "Brigadier General Mercer to General Washington, 9 July, 1776," 251

[9] Ibid.

[10] Ibid.

to confer with Major Thomas Knowlton of Connecticut about harassing the enemy on Staten Island with small raids. Knowlton had been posted on Bergen Neck with the 20th Continental Regiment (Connecticut troops) since the spring and had reconnoitered Staten Island several times. General Washington hoped that with enemy operations soon to commence, a surprise American raid upon Staten Island would, "*alarm the Enemy & encourage our own Troops who seem generally desirous something should be done*."[11]

General Mercer, who was appointed by Washington on July 14th, to command the Flying Camp, informed the commander in chief that as soon as a sufficient number of troops arrived, he would strike out across the water to "*surprise the Enemies small posts*," on Staten Island.[12]

Just such a move was attempted four days later on the evening of July 18th. Thirteen hundred Pennsylvania troops assembled near Elizabethtown with the intention to cross the Arthur Kill to Staten Island and attack an estimated five to six hundred enemy troops posted along the western side of the island in three locations.[13] Mercer disappointingly reported that

> *Very tempestuous weather coming on, obliged us to desist altogether from the enterprise, some gentlemen, being well acquainted with the passage there, being of opinion that we should endanger the*

---

[11] Ibid., "War Council, 12 July, 1776," 280

[12] Ibid., "Brigadier General Mercer to General Washington 14 July, 1776," 309

[13] Force, ed., "General Mercer to the President of Congress, 20 July, 1776," *American Archives*, Fifth Series, Volume 1, 469

loss of our whole party in attempting to cross in such boats as we were provided with.[14]

General Mercer informed General Washington that more troops and the passage of time were needed before another attempt to raid Staten Island from New Jersey was made:

It cannot be renewed till we have more Forces here – nor would it be prudent to attempt any Surprize for some days – as our motions are probably communicated to the Enemy.[15]

Within days of the abortive raid on Staten Island, Mercer's force in New Jersey more than doubled thanks to the arrival of several battalions of militia from Pennsylvania. Some of the men who arrived were Mercer's former comrades in the French and Indian War like Colonel James Burd, who brought hundreds of Pennsylvania militia from Cumberland County with him.

With over 3,000 troops posted from Perth Amboy to Bergen Neck and reports of more on the march, Mercer found himself short of muskets.[16] He informed General Washington that twelve foot long pikes were provided to some of the men who arrived with no weapons.[17]

The remainder of July passed quietly for General Mercer and his troops. They fired a few ineffective artillery rounds at

---

[14] Ibid.

[15] Chase, ed., "Brigadier General Mercer to General Washington 19 July, 1776," *The Papers of George Washington,* Vol. 5, 388

[16] Force, ed., "A General Return of the Troops in New Jersey… 25 July, 1776," *American Archives*, Fifth Series, Vol. 1, 574

[17] Chase, ed., "Brigadier General Mercer to General Washington 24 July, 1776," *The Papers of George Washington,* Vol. 5, 444

several small British boats that passed into Raritan Bay and grumbled about the quality of their provisions. The complaints prompted General Mercer to request that General Washington intervene as quickly as possible.[18] Mercer reminded Washington (who was no doubt already fully aware) of, "*how essential it is that no cause of complaint be given to troops in our present circumstances….*"[19] This was especially true for militia, who were always eager to return to their homes and quick to find any reason to do so.

Although the number of Pennsylvania militia serving in New Jersey had grown significantly in July, few of them were actually attached to the Flying Camp. In fact, in early August General Mercer informed Congress that only 274 troops, "*properly belonging to the Flying Camp, have yet joined.*"[20] This did not include a battalion of troops from Maryland under Colonel William Smallwood who was posted in Elizabethtown and assigned to the Flying Camp (but were destined to be sent to General Washington's army in New York).

Smallwood's Maryland troops would not be the only ones detached from New Jersey to reinforce General Washington in New York. With only 10,514 men fit for duty in New York in early August, Washington desperately needed reinforcements and instructed General Mercer to detach 2,000 troops from the Flying Camp.[21] Washington informed Congress of his request.

---

[18] Ibid., "Brigadier General Mercer to General Washington 29 July, 1776," 504-505

[19] Ibid.

[20] Force, ed., "General Mercer to the President of Congress, 4 August, 1776," *American Archives*, Fifth Series, Vol. 1, 750

[21] Chase, ed., "General Washington to John Hancock, 8-9 August, 1776," *The Papers of George Washington,* Vol. 5, 627

> *I have wrote to Genl Mercer for Two Thousand men from the Flying Camp: Colo. Smallwood's Battalion as part of them I expect this forenoon, But where the rest are to come from, I know not, as by the Genl's last return, nor more than three or four hundred of the New Levies had got in.*[22]

Although General Mercer had few troops to spare from the Flying Camp, several thousand militia were also under his command in New Jersey and he sent as many as he could to New York. Two battalions of Pennsylvania riflemen (700 strong) under Colonel Samuel Miles and a battalion of Pennsylvania militia under Colonel Samuel Atlee were ordered to New York on August 10th.[23] The next day, Mercer informed Washington that

> *About Twelve hundred Spears are sent off agreeable to your orders... I shall push on as many of the Flying Camp & Volunteers as possible but cannot as yet ascertain the Number.*[24]

General Mercer informed Washington the following day that another battalion of militia, with a company of riflemen, was on the way, and that he intended to, "*have ready at New Ark as expeditiously as possible Two Thousand men – to reinforce the Army at New York – if you think their Services there necessary.*"[25] In addition to the troops in Newark, General Mercer assured Washington that the posts on the Jersey shore opposite Staten Island were, "*sufficiently*

---

[22] Ibid.
[23] Ibid., "General Mercer, to General Washington, 10 August, 1776," 659
[24] Ibid., "General Mercer to General Washington, 11 August, 1776," 666
[25] Ibid., "General Mercer to General Washington, 12 August, 1776," 685

guarded," and with more troops arriving daily, Mercer asked permission to post 400 men at Powles Hook and 500 men at Bergen Town.[26]

A few days later Mercer informed Washington that he had increased the number of troops at Bergen Town to a thousand. He also informed Washington that his old regiment, the 3rd Virginia, was on the march north and asked whether they should remain with the Flying Camp in New Jersey or proceed to New York.[27] It would be another month before Mercer's brother in law and successor in the 3rd Virginia, Colonel George Weedon, arrived, but when he and his troops did, General Washington posted them on Manhattan Island.

In the meantime, amidst numerous signs of an impending British attack, General Mercer guarded the New Jersey shore in August with 799 troops in Perth Amboy, 605 troops in Woodbridge, 982 troops in Elizabethtown, and 2,534 troops at Fort Constitution (present day Fort Lee).[28] This last post was under construction and was to work in conjunction with another fort across the Hudson River on Manhattan Island (Fort Washington) to prevent British warships from sailing upriver. While the troops at Fort Constitution worked to erect fortifications overlooking the Hudson River, General Howe directed his efforts against Long Island and ultimately New York City.

---

[26] Philander D. Chase and Frank E. Grizzard, eds., "General Mercer to General Washington, 15 August, 1776," *The Papers of George Washington,* Vol. 6, (Charlottesville, VA: University Press of Virginia, 1994), 32

[27] Ibid., "General Mercer to General Washington,19 August, 1776," 78

[28] Force, ed., "General Return of the Army in New Jersey under the command of General Mercer, 20 August, 1776," *American Archives,* Fifth Series, Vol. 1, 1079

Long Island: Battle and Retreat

On the morning of August 27th, heavy cannon and musket fire could be heard by General Mercer and his troops far to the east on Long Island. The Battle of Long Island had commenced. Initially it seemed that Washington's outnumbered troops might do well. They held a strong position along Gowanus Heights and appeared to have repulsed an enemy frontal assault at the start of the engagement. When it was discovered that half of the British army had swung around the American left flank and gotten in their rear, however, General Washington's troops broke and ran. Hundreds of Americans were killed, wounded and captured and the shattered survivors scrambled towards the incomplete American lines on Brooklyn Heights.

At some point in the engagement, General Washington ordered General Mercer to send reinforcements to New York via Powles Hook. Mercer informed Congress that

> *General Washington had wrote me that some reinforcements would be necessary at New York and Powles Hook; such troops as composed or were enlisted for the Flying Camp were ordered to proceed immediately for* [Powles Hook]. *On the way yesterday evening, General Wooster's Aid-de-Camp met me, with a few lines from the General, signifying it was General Washington's orders that I should march, with all our Army under my command, immediately to Powles Hook. The necessary orders were sent to Amboy, Woodbridge, and Elizabeth Town and I hope to have on Bergen, ready to pass*

> *over to New York, if required, from three to four thousand men.*[29]

Mercer added that his entire force in New Jersey amounted to 8,300 men, but many, "*have joined us with arms unfit for service, and some have refused to march on.*"[30]

Back on Long Island, General Washington scrambled to restore order to his shattered army. He received a lucky break when General Howe opted not to storm the weak American works at Brooklyn Heights but instead, take them by siege. This allowed Washington an opportunity to evacuate his troops from Long Island and he did so on the evening of August 30th.

With his ability to hold New York in doubt, General Washington wrote a candid letter to Congress blasting the conduct of the militia:

> *Our situation is truly distressing – The check our Detachment sustained on the 27th* [of August] *has dispirited too great a proportion of our Troops and filled their minds with apprehension and despair – The Militia instead of calling forth their utmost efforts to a brave & manly opposition in order to repair our Losses, are dismayed, Intractable, and Impatient to return. Great numbers of them have gone off; in some Instances, almost by whole Regiments – by half Ones & by Companies at a time.*[31]

---

[29] Ibid., "General Mercer to the President of Congress, 28 August, 1776," 1193

[30] Ibid.

[31] Chase and Grizzard, eds., "General Washington to John Hancock, 2 September, 1776," *The Papers of George Washington,* Vol. 6, 199

Washington lamented that the militia's poor example had infected the rest of the army:

> *When their want of discipline & refusal of almost every kind of restraint & Government, have produced a like conduct...and an entire disregard of that order and subordination necessary to the well doing of an Army...I am obliged to confess my want of confidence in the Generality of the Troops.*[32]

Just two days later, General Mercer expressed similar concerns to Congress about the militia:

> *On a general view of our force, compared with that of the enemy, the event of this campaign is...greatly to be dreaded. General Washington has not, so far as I have seen, five thousand men to be depended on for the service of a campaign, and I have not one thousand. Both our armies are composed of raw Militia, perpetually fluctuating between the camp and their farms. Poorly armed and still worse disciplined, these, sir, are not a match, even were their numbers equal, which they are not, for veteran troops, well fitted, and urged on by able officers.*[33]

The quality of the militia officers was evidently of some concern to Mercer for he added that, *"giving soldiers, or even the lower orders of mankind, the choice of officers, will forever mar the discipline of your armies.*"[34]

---

[32] Ibid.
[33] Force, ed., "General Mercer to the President of Congress, 4 September, 1776," *American Archives,* Fifth Series, Vol. 2, 157
[34] Ibid.

Fall of New York

The day before General Mercer expressed these sentiments, General Washington ordered Mercer to send a strong detachment to Fort Constitution to strengthen this important post.[35] General Washington hoped that the cannon at Fort Constitution, in conjunction with a number of river obstacles (sunken ships and chevaux de frise) and the cannon at Fort Washington (which sat across thc rivcr on Manhattan Island) would prevent British ships from passing up the Hudson River to trap Washington's army on Manhattan Island. The danger of that happening was very real and was discussed by Washington and his generals at a September 7th war council. The American commander-in-chief believed that

> *It is now extremely obvious from all Intelligence* [that]...*they mean to inclose us on the Island of New York by taking post in our Rear,* [at King's Bridge] *while the Shipping effectually secure the Front; and thus either by cutting off our Communication with the Country oblige us to fight them on their own Terms or Surrender at discretion, or by a Brilliant stroke endeavor to cut this Army to pieces & secure the collection of Arms & Stores which they know we shall not be able soon to replace.*[36]

---

[35] Chase and Grizzard, eds., "General Washington to General Mercer, 2 September, 1776," *The Papers of George Washington,* Vol. 6, 209

[36] Ibid., "General Washington to John Hancock, 8 September, 1776," 248-49

Yet, Washington, on the advice of a majority of officers present, decided to maintain a large number of troops in New York, asserting that

> *To abandon a City which has been by some deemed defensible and on whose Works much Labor has been bestowed has a tendency to dispirit the Troops and enfeeble our Cause.*[37]

To avoid demoralizing the army any further, General Washington decided to keep 5,000 troops in New York. Another 9,000 were posted to protect King's Bridge, on the opposite end of Manhattan.[38] The remainder of Washington's army was posted between the city and King's Bridge, ready to support either end of the island.

Illness and an errant messenger prevented General Mercer from attending the council of war. He offered his views to Washington in a letter, instead. Mercer emphasized the importance of preventing a junction between General Howe's army in New York and Canadian Governor Guy Carleton's army (that was advancing south down Lake Champlain from Canada). Mercer also agreed that New York City should continue to be defended to deny the enemy comfortable quarters for as long as possible.[39] Mercer offered a bit of hope to Washington as well by asserting that

---

[37] Ibid.

[38] Ibid.

[39] Ibid., "General Mercer to General Washington, 7 September, 1776," 243

> *I hope to be able very soon to effect some enterprize on Staten Island – when we have a Sufficient Number of men for the Flying Camp to dispose along the different Posts – but the Militia are not the Men for such a Purpose – Four Colonels were with me some Nights ago to inform that their men would fight the Enemy on this Side – but would not go over Staten Island.*[40]

Alas, another month passed before General Mercer was capable of launching a raid on Staten Island. In the meantime, General Washington reversed his decision to defend New York City and began the process of re-deploying the army to Harlem Heights on the northern end of Manhattan Island.[41]

On the morning of September 15th, before the withdrawal from New York was complete, British troops landed on the eastern side of Manhattan a few miles above New York at Kip's Bay. The Americans posted there offered little resistance; most panicked and fled north towards Harlem Heights. Luckily, the bulk of Washington's troops still in New York managed to escape along the west side of Manhattan. They fled north to join their comrades at Harlem Heights. Once again, General Washington's troops, particularly the militia, performed poorly in the field and New York City fell easily to the British.

General Mercer understood completely the frustrations of relying on the militia to defend a post. While the bulk of Howe's forces concentrated on capturing Manhattan, British

---

[40] Ibid., 243-44

[41] Ibid., "General Washington to John Hancock, 11 September, 1776," 209

warships bombarded Mercer's troops at Powles Hook and Bergen. Mercer complained to General Washington that

> *The Melitia of Pennsylva. and New Jersey stationed on Bergen and at Powlis Hook have behaved in a scandalous Manner – running off from their Posts on the first Cannonade from the Ships of the Enemy – At all the Posts we find it difficult to keep the Melitia to their duty.*[42]

General Mercer's complaints about the militia continued into the next day with a second letter to General Washington.

> *Such is the ever fluctuating State of our Melitia and infamous Desertion – that we are not at any one Post two days in the same State as to Numbers.*[43]

Mercer's frustration was understandable. Charged with defending New Jersey from a sudden British attack, General Mercer had detachments of militia posted from Perth Amboy (his main encampment) to Fort Constitution, 30 miles to the northeast. It was a daunting challenge to maintain this scattered force of militia. Fortunately, General Washington eased Mercer's burden a bit by sending General Nathanael Greene and a brigade of Massachusetts continentals under General John Nixon to reinforce Fort Constitution.

With Fort Constitution now under General Greene's authority, Mercer turned his attention to Powles Hook, just a mile and a half across the Hudson River from New York.

---

[42] Ibid., "General Mercer to General Washington, 17 September, 1776," 327

[43] Ibid., "General Mercer to General Washington, 18 September, 1776," 339

Realizing that the British were preparing to seize Powles Hook and that he was powerless to stop them, Mercer spared his men and evacuated the post, leaving a small guard which fled when the British attacked on September 23rd.[44] The British incursion into New Jersey was not the beginning of a general movement in that direction but rather, a move to secure New York Harbor (given the proximity of Powles Hook to it) from rebel harassment. General Howe's attention remained locked on Washington's army to the north, and on October 12th, after three weeks of relative inactivity, Howe finally acted to confront the rebels.

Throg's Neck

General Washington's position on the northern end of Manhattan Island was strong. This was evidenced by a victorious skirmish with the British at Harlem Heights on September 16th, a victory that involved General Mercer's brother-in-law, Colonel Weedon and the 3rd Virginia. Weedon's success at Harlem Heights temporarily boosted American morale.

Determined to avoid the casualties that an all-out frontal assault against Harlem Heights would inflict on his men, General Howe looked to outmaneuver Washington and strike him from behind. On October 12th, British troops landed on Throng's Neck, a peninsula that extended from the mainland into Long Island Sound, just a few miles east of Harlem Heights. Howe planned to sweep ashore and march west to capture King's Bridge, severing Washington's supply and

---

[44] Richard K. Showman, ed., "General Greene to General Washington, 23 September, 1776," *The Papers of General Nathanael Greene*, Vol. 1, (Chapel Hill: University of North Carolina Press, 1976), 302-03

escape route off Manhattan. Then Howe could attack the Americans at Harlem Heights from multiple directions and destroy them. The operation proved difficult as American resistance at Throg's Neck delayed the British on the peninsula.

General Washington took advantage of Howe's delay and removed the bulk of his troops from Manhattan. He left 1,200 men to defend Fort Washington, but marched north with the rest of the army towards White Plains. Washington explained his actions to Congress:

> *We are again obliged to change our disposition to counteract the Operations of the Enemy declining an Attack upon our Front, they have drawn the main body of their Army to Frogs point with a design of Hemming us in, and drawing a line in our Rear. To prevent the consequences which would... probably follow the execution of their Scheme, the General Officers determined Yesterday that our forces must be taken from hence, and extended towards East & West Chester so as to out flank them.*[45]

While General Washington redeployed his army, General Mercer acted to assist Washington and divert Howe's attention back to Staten Island.

---

[45] Chase and Grizzard, eds., "Lt. Col. Robert Hanson Harrison to John Hancock, 14-17 October, 1776, " *The Papers of George Washington,* Vol. 6, 565

Mercer's Raid on Staten Island

General Mercer had waited for weeks for a chance to attack the British on Staten Island and he finally resolved to do so on October 15th . He described the operation to Congress:

> *In the night of the 15th, General Greene passed over with me to Staten Island, with part of the troops at this post* [Perth-Amboy]. *We were to be joined on the march by the Jersey Militia from the Blazing Star* [Ferry], *Elizabeth-Town, and Newark. Our intention was to reach the east end of the island by break of day, and attack the enemy, where we understood their greatest force lay. If successful there, the smaller posts would yield of course.*[46]

Around midnight, General Greene received orders from General Washington to report to Fort Washington immediately. Greene complied and returned to New Jersey, leaving General Mercer to lead the attack. Mercer recalled that

> *I was then advanced within a few miles of Richmond town,* [on Staten Island] *and received information on the march that a company of British troops, one of Hessians, and one of* [Tory] *militia, lay there. Reducing that post was, therefore, our first object. Colonel Griffin was detached, with Colonel Patterson's battalion, and Major Clarke, at the head of some Riflemen, to fall in upon the east end of the*

---

[46] Force, ed., "General Mercer to the President of Congress, 17 October, 1776," *American Archives,* Fifth Series, Vol. 2, 1093

> *town, while the remainder of the troops enclosed it on the other quarters. Both divisions reached the town by break of day, but not before the enemy were alarmed. Most of them fled, after exchanging a few shot with Colonel Griffin's detachment. Two soldiers were mortally wounded, and seventeen taken prisoner, with the loss on our side of two soldiers killed* [and a handful wounded.][47]

The discovery of Mercer's troops on their approach undermined his attack and left the general disappointed. Withdrawing back to New Jersey, Mercer shared his disappointment with General Washington, noting that, "*Well disciplined Troops would have taken the whole without the loss of a man – but we only took about twenty prisoners, partly Hessian & English.*"[48]

General Mercer had little time to dwell on his disappointment; orders from General Washington arrived instructing Mercer to re-organize the troops in New Jersey.

White Plains

While General Mercer, in cooperation with General Greene at newly named Fort Lee (formerly Fort Constitution) worked to re-organize the troops in New Jersey, General Washington marched to White Plains and prepared to confront General Howe. Over a week passed before Howe moved against Washington and when he did so, only a portion of the two armies actually clashed (on October 28th) at Chatterton Hill.

---

[47] Ibid.

[48] Chase and Grizzard, eds., "General Mercer to General Washington, 16 October, 1776," *The Papers of George Washington,* Vol. 6, 577

Continental troops from Delaware and Maryland, along with militia forces, stubbornly defended the hill and inflicted a number of casualties on Howe's troops. The weight of the British attack was too great, however, and the Americans withdrew from the hill.

Pleased with the day's gains, General Howe halted his army and waited for reinforcements. He attempted to advance two days later, but poor weather postponed the move. When the skies cleared on November 1st, General Howe discovered that Washington had withdrawn to an even stronger position five miles to the north. Howe declined to pursue and instead, marched west to Dobb's Ferry on the east bank of the Hudson River. Concerned that New Jersey was Howe's target, General Washington ordered two divisions of his army (essentially all of the troops from states south of New York) to cross the Hudson at Peekskill and reinforce New Jersey.[49]

General Mercer, who marched a portion of the Flying Camp from Perth Amboy to Fort Lee, was ordered by General Greene to take command of the troops posted at Sneed's Landing, directly across from Dobb's Ferry. Mercer was instructed , "*to have everything removed out of the Enemies way – particularly Cattle, Carriages, Hay & Grain.*"[50] This proved to be unnecessary because General Howe suddenly marched his army south towards the last remaining American post on Manhattan.

---

[49] Chase and Grizzard, eds., "General Washington to John Hancock, 9 November, 1776," *The Papers of George Washington,* Vol. 7, (Charlottesville, VA: University Press of Virginia, 1997), 121

[50] Ibid., "General Greene to General Washington, 10 November, 1776," 131

Fort Washington

Fort Washington, built on a 230 foot elevation overlooking the Hudson River, was originally constructed to challenge British shipping on the river. It was one component of the American defenses at Harlem Heights. When General Washington moved the bulk of his army to White Plains in mid-October, Fort Washington became the bastion of the reduced American presence on Manhattan. Despite General Washington's doubts about the value and security of the fort he accepted the advice of General Nathanael Greene and maintained a garrison there. General Greene explained the importance of Fort Washington in a letter to General Washington:

> *Upon the whole I cannot help thinking the Garrison* [Fort Washington] *is of advantage – and I cannot conceive the Garrison to be in any great danger the men can be brought off at any time…Col. Magaw* [Fort Washington's commander] *thinks it will take* [the enemy] *till December expires, before they can carry it* [the fort]*…If the Enemy don't find it an Object of importance they won't trouble themselves about it -- if they do, it is full proof they feel an injury from our possessing it – Our giving it up will open a free communication with the Country by the Way of Kings bridge – that must be a great Advantage to them and injury to us.*[51]

---

[51] Ibid. "General Nathaniel Greene to General Washington, 9 November, 1776," 120

Colonel Robert Magaw commanded the 1,200 man garrison at Fort Washington. Although this contingent was adequate to defend the fort, it was far short of the manpower necessary to properly defend the approaches to the fort. General Greene rushed reinforcements (which included hundreds of troops from Mercer's Flying Camp) across the river at the last minute to increase the garrison to nearly 2,900 men, but this was still far too few to oppose the 8,000 troops that General Howe sent against Fort Washington on November 16th.[52]

General Mercer was actually with General Washington and General Greene, making their way across the Hudson River to inspect Fort Washington when the British attack commenced. General Greene recalled that

> *General Washington, General Putnam, General Mercer and myself went to the Island* [from Fort Lee] *to determine what was best to be done, but Just at the instant we stept on board the Boat the Enemy made their appearance on the Hill...and began a severe Cannonade....* [53]

Despite the danger, the American commanders proceeded across the river. General Greene continued:

---

[52] K.G. Davies, ed., *Documents of the American Revolution,* Vol. 12, (Irish University Press, 1976), 258
and Barnet Schecter, *The Battle of New York: The City at the Heart of the American Revolution,* (New York: Walker & Company, 2002), 247

[53] Showman, ed., General Greene to General Washington, 23 September, 1776," *The Papers of General Nathanael Greene*, Vol. 1, 302-03

There we all stood in a very awkward situation; as the disposition was made and the Enemy advancing we durst not attempt to make any new disposition – indeed we saw nothing amiss. We all urged his Excellency to come off. I offerd to stay. General Putnam did the same and so did General Mercer, but his Excellency thought it best for us all to come off together, which we did about half an hour before the Enemy surrounded the fort.[54]

The battle for Fort Washington lasted but a few hours. Although Howe's troops suffered hundreds of casualties in their approach to Fort Washington, the fort was too small to protect the large number of rebel defenders that sought safety behind its walls. To avoid a slaughter, Colonel Magaw relented to British demands for an immediate surrender and before the day ended over 2,800 Americans were prisoners of war.[55]

The loss of Fort Washington was a devastating blow to the American cause. General Washington lamented to Congress that

The Loss of such a Number of Officers and Men, many of whom have been trained with more than common Attention, will I fear be severely felt. But when that of the Arms and Accoutrements is added much more so….[56]

---

[54] Ibid.
[55] Davies, ed., *Documents of the American Revolution,* Vol. 12, 258
[56] Chase and Grizzard, eds. "General Washington to John Hancock, 16 November, 1776," *The Papers of George Washington,* Vol. 7, 165

The loss of Fort Washington eliminated the effectiveness (limited as it was) of Fort Lee as an obstacle to British navigation on the Hudson River. General Washington wasted no time in ordering the military stores that had accumulated at Fort Lee to be moved westward as a precaution against a possible British strike across the Hudson.

General Mercer proceeded to Elizabethtown to prepare the remnants of the Flying Camp posted at Perth Amboy, Woodbridge, and Elizabethtown for action. He did not have to wait long.

Chapter Five

"We Have Much Need for a Speedy Re-inforcement"

The Long Retreat

November – December 1776

On November 20th, just four days after the fall of Fort Washington, General Howe sent a large British force under General Lord Charles Cornwallis across the Hudson River to attack Fort Lee. Although General Washington had anticipated this move, a significant amount of military stores remained in the fort, most of which were abandoned upon word that the enemy was on its way. General Washington reported to Congress that the garrison successfully retreated to Hackensack (four miles to the west) but

> *We lost the whole of the Cannon that was at the Fort, except Two twelve Pounders, and a great deal of baggage – between Two & three hundred Tents – about a Thousand Barrells of Flour & other Stores....*[1]

[1] Chase and Grizzard, eds., "General Washington to John Hancock, 19-21 November, 1776," *The Papers of George Washington,* Vol. 7, 183

From Hackensack, Washington instructed General Mercer in Elizabethtown to, "*hold yourself in readiness to march at a moment's warning*," and to pass this instruction on to General Adam Stephen and Lord Stirling (both of who commanded brigades in New Jersey).[2] Washington resumed his march southwestward the next day, moving four miles to Acquackanonk Landing to cross the Passaic River. The Americans then marched south about nine miles to Newark, where Washington halted to await Cornwallis's next move.[3]

General Cornwallis followed Washington to Hackensack where he halted for a few days to consolidate his forces. Cornwallis knew that the American army was divided and that General Charles Lee could suddenly appear on his flank or rear with several thousand rebel troops. The British commander did not realize that despite numerous appeals from General Washington to bring his force to New Jersey, General Lee and his troops remained in New York for the rest of November.

Although Lee's conduct in this period has been criticized by many who think Lee actually wanted Washington and his bedraggled army to be defeated so that Lee could assume command of the remaining American forces, Cornwallis's uncertainty about Lee's whereabouts and intentions in late November actually restrained British movements. Cornwallis was wary of a sudden strike from Lee on his flank or rear and acted with an abundance of caution in his pursuit of Washington.

---

[2] Ibid., "William Grayson to General Mercer, 20 November, 1776, " note 10, 186

[3] Ibid., "General Washington to John Hancock,19-21 November, 1776," 183

General Cornwallis did not proceed to Acquackanonk Landing until November 26th, five days after Washington passed there. He then marched south (after two nights at Acquackanonk) and continued to Newark, arriving on November 28th. Cornwallis's approach forced Washington to resume his retreat. He ordered General Mercer, who had remained in Elizabethtown with the Flying Camp, to rendezvous with him in New Brunswick.

Heavy rain made the roads nearly impassable, but the outnumbered Americans had little choice. All of Washington's officers were in agreement that

> *A retreat to* [New Brunswick] *was requisite and founded in necessity, as our force was by no means sufficient to make a stand against the Enemy, much superior in number, with the least probability of success, & whose advanced Guards were entering* [Newark] *by the time our Rear got out.*[4]

Captain John Chilton of General Mercer's old 3rd Virginia Regiment was in the rear of Washington's army and described the march to New Brunswick:

> *This was a melancholy day,* [November 27] *deep miry road and so many men to tread it made it very disagreeable marching, we came 8 or 10 miles and encamped....How long we shall stay, I can't say, but expect we shall make a stand near this place* [New Brunswick] *if not at it, but no certainty when the Enemy are advancing on and an engagement may*

---

[4] Ibid., "General Washington to John Hancock, 30 November, 1776," 232

> *happen before tomorrow night. We must fight to a disadvantage. They exceed us in numbers greatly.*[5]

Unfortunately, General Mercer's Flying Camp offered little relief to the shortage of troops at New Brunswick; the enlistments of most of Mercer's men expired at the end of November. Despite the pleadings of General Washington, General Mercer, and their officers, two entire brigades of militia, (the bulk from General Mercer's command) left the American ranks on December 1st, and headed home.[6] This left Washington with less than 4,000 men in New Brunswick fit for service to face an enemy nearly twice as large.[7] Sergeant James McMichael, with the Pennsylvania state rifle regiment, captured the sentiment of the remaining troops in his diary:

> *Intelligence that the enemy are marching for Brunswick causing us to prepare to meet them but we are reduced to so small a number we have little hopes of victory.*[8]

Although the loss of the Flying Camp was a blow to the army, General Washington valued Mercer's leadership and immediately assigned him another command. General Mercer

---

[5] Lyon Tyler, "John Chilton to his brother, 30 November, 1776," *Tyler's Quarterly Historical and Genealogical Magazine,* Vol. 12, (Richmond, VA: Richmond Press Inc., 1931), 98

[6] Showman, ed., "General Greene to Governor Cooke, 4 December, 1776," *The Papers of General Nathanael Greene*, Vol. 1, 362

[7] Force, ed. "General Return of the Army, Trenton, December 1, 1776," *American Archives*, Series 5, Vol. 3, 1035 and
Chase and Grizzard, eds., "General Washington to John Hancock, 1 December, 1776," *The Papers of George Washington,* Vol. 7, 243

[8] "Diary of Lieutenant James McMichael of the Pennsylvania Line 1776-1778," *Pennsylvania Magazine of History and Biography,* Vol. 16, No. 2, (1892), 139

was placed in charge of a brigade consisting of three continental regiments (the 20th Regiment from Connecticut, the 27th Regiment from Massachusetts, and the 1st Maryland Regiment) as well as a regiment of Connecticut state troops (militia) and the remnants of Colonel Moses Rawlings Maryland and Virginia rifle corps. Mercer's brigade amounted to approximately 1,000 men and accounted for over a quarter of the force with General Washington.[9] They marched with the rest of Washington's army towards Princeton on the evening of December 1st (bivouacking along the road) and reached Princeton the following morning. Many had hoped to find General Lee at Princeton (or at least intelligence about his whereabouts) but Lee's location and destination remained a mystery to Washington and his men.

Washington's troops enjoyed a brief reprieve from the chase when General Cornwallis halted in New Brunswick for a few days to await the arrival of General Howe and reinforcements. Washington used the respite to transport his baggage across the Delaware River at Trenton. Two brigades (Stirling's and Stephen's) remained in Princeton to, "*watch the Motions of the Enemy and give Notice of their Approach*," while General Mercer's and General Fermoy's brigades moved the baggage and military stores into Pennsylvania.[10]

On December 5th, Washington reported to Congress that the bulk of his baggage had been passed over the river:

---

[9] Force, ed. "General Return of the Army, Trenton, December 1, 1776," *American Archives*, Fifth Series, Vol. 3, 1035

[10] Chase and Grizzard, eds., "General Washington to John Hancock, 3 December, 1776," *The Papers of George Washington*, Vol. 7, 255

> *I shall now, having removed the greatest part of the* [baggage], *face about with such Troops as are here fit for service, and march back to Princeton and there govern myself by circumstances and the movements of Genl Lee.*[11]

Mercer's brigade was sent back to Princeton and deployed east of town along the road to New Brunswick.[12] Their stay was brief, for on December 7th, General Cornwallis, accompanied by General Howe, finally left New Brunswick to resume his "pursuit" of Washington.

General Washington received the news of Cornwallis's approach while proceeding back to Princeton from Trenton. He recounted to Congress that

> *Before I got* [to Princeton] *I received a Second express informing me, that as the Enemy were advancing by different Routs and attempting by One to get in the rear of our Troops which were there & whose numbers were small and the place by no means defensible, they had judged it prudent to retreat to Trenton.*[13]

Washington immediately reversed direction and returned to Trenton to prepare to transport the army across the river. Behind him marched General Mercer and the other brigades that had guarded Princeton.

Charles Wilson Peale, a lieutenant in the Pennsylvania Militia (and noted artist), arrived in Trenton on December 7th

---

[11] Ibid., "General Washington to John Hancock, 5 December, 1776," 262
[12] Ibid., "General Greene to General Washington, 7 December, 1776," 268
[13] Ibid., "General Washington to John Hancock, 8 December, 1776," 273

to reinforce Washington and joined the army's withdrawal across the river.[14] He recalled years later in his autobiography that

> *Genl. Washington's whole army...made a grand, but dreadfull appearance. All the shores were lighted up with large fires. The Boats continually passing and repassing, full of men, Horses, artillery and camp Equipage. The* [hollering] *of hundreds of men in their difficulties of getting Horses and artillery out of the boats, made it rather the appearance of Hell than any earthly scene. That night* [we] *lay...by a fire on the shore....*[15]

Lieutenant Peale discovered his brother the next day among the ranks of one of General Mercer's units, the 1st Maryland Regiment. Peale described their reunion:

> *James...had been in the rear guard, through all the retreat of the American Army from the north River, and had lost all of his clothes. He was in an Old dirty Blanket-Jacket, his beard long, and his face so full of sores that he could not clean it, which disfigured him in such a manner that he was not known by* [me] *at first sight.*[16]

Months earlier, Lieutenant Peale's brother, James, had marched to New York with Colonel William Smallwood's 1st

---

[14] "Journal of Charles Wilson Peale," 7 December, 1776, *Pennsylvania Magazine of History and Biography*, Vol. 38, (Philadelphia: The Historical Society of Pennsylvania, 1914), 271

[15] Sidney Hart, ed., *The Selected Papers of Charles Wilson Peale and his family, Volume 5, The Autobiography of Charles Wilson Peale,* (New Haven and London: Yale University Press, 2000), 50

[16] Ibid.

Maryland Regiment. Over the course of the campaign in New York and New Jersey, Smallwood's unit suffered heavy losses and had dwindled to just over 200 effectives by early December.[17] Lieutenant Peale visited the 1st Maryland's campsite and found the troops, "*scattered through the woods in huts made of poles, straw, leaves, etc. in a dirty ragged condition*."[18] Their situation and condition was typical for most of Washington's army.

General Washington had previously ordered all of the boats in the area seized to prevent their use by the enemy, but the danger remained that some were overlooked, or that the British might build rafts or bring their own boats to cross the Delaware, so Washington's troops had to remain vigilant and guard the crossing points of the river. General Washington took the added precaution to warn Congress of the real possibility of an enemy attack on Philadelphia:

> *I am led to think, that the Enemy are bringing Boats with them, if so, it will be impossible for our small Force to give them any considerable Opposition in the Passage of the River.... Under these Circumstances, the Security of Philadelphia should be our next Object.*[19]

Washington advised that earthworks be built to defend the approaches to Philadelphia and additional troops raised as soon as possible to protect the de facto capital.

---

[17] Force, ed. "General Return of the Army, Trenton, December 1, 1776," *American Archives*, Fifth Series, Vol. 3, 1035

[18] "Journal of Charles Wilson Peale, 9 December, 1776," *Pennsylvania Magazine of History and Biography*, Vol. 38, 273

[19] Chase and Grizzard, eds., "General Washington to John Hancock, 9 December, 1776," *The Papers of George Washington,* Vol. 7, 283

While much of Philadelphia panicked (and Congress fled to Baltimore) at the news that the British had reached the Delaware River, Washington and his men guarded the river crossings as best they could. For a few days it appeared that the British intended to cross the river (or at least attempt to) somewhere above Trenton. A captured British soldier informed Washington on December 11th, that Lord Cornwallis was at Pennington, eight miles north of Trenton, with a large body of troops.[20] Scouts from General Stirling's brigade reported that Cornwallis had actually marched beyond Pennington to Coryell's Ferry on the Delaware River, but could not obtain boats to cross so they marched back to Pennington to await further orders.[21] The possibility that the enemy might soon find the means to cross the Delaware worried General Washington. He deployed his troops along the west bank of the river, but his small numbers made it difficult to cover every possible crossing point. Washington explained the challenge he faced to Lund Washington, his relative and the caretaker of Mount Vernon during General Washington's absence:

> *We have brought over, and destroyed, all the Boats we could lay our hands on, upon the Jersey Shore for many Miles above and below this place* [across from Trenton]; *but it is next to impossible to guard a Shore for 60 Miles with less than half the Enemys numbers; when by force, or Stratagem they may suddenly attempt a passage in many different places. At*

---

[20] Ibid., "General Washington to John Hancock, 11 December, 1776," 296-97

[21] Ibid., 297

> *present they are Incamp'd or quartered along the other shore above and below us...for fifteen Miles.*[22]

Washington's challenge was eased somewhat when 2,000 Pennsylvania militia arrived to reinforce his army.[23] Washington posted them between Bristol (ten miles downriver from Trenton) and Yardley's Ferry (three miles upriver from Trenton). General Mercer's brigade was posted a few miles above Yardley's Ferry, near McConkey's Ferry, and the brigades of General Stephen and General Stirling guarded the crossing points further upriver all the way to Coryell's Ferry.[24]

General Washington instructed General Mercer and his fellow brigade commanders to be vigilant on their watch of the river and, if the enemy should cross, "*give* [them] *all the Opposition they possibly can,*" without waiting for orders from Washington.[25] The American commander-in-chief stressed that, "*Everything in a manner depends upon the defense at the Water's Edge,*" and he urged each brigade commander to send spies across the river to collect intelligence on the enemy's situation and intentions.[26] For the time being, General Howe seemed content to fire a few sporadic cannon shots at the Americans while Howe's troops searched for a way to cross the river.

---

[22] Ibid., "General Washington to Lund Washington, 10-17 December, 1776," 291

[23] Ibid., "General Washington to Samuel Washington, 18 December, 1776," 370

[24] Ibid., "General Orders, 12 December, 1776," 303

[25] Ibid., "General Washington to Brigadier Generals James Ewing, Hugh Mercer, Adam Stephen, and Lord Stirling, 14 December, 1776," 332

[26] Ibid.

"The Game is Pretty Near Up"

Lacking proper shelter and winter clothing, Washington's men stood watch along the banks of the Delaware River during the cold days and nights of December. Lieutenant Enoch Anderson of the Delaware Regiment (which was attached to General Stirling's brigade) recalled that

> We *lay amongst the leaves without tents or blankets, laying down with our feet to the fire. It was very cold. We had meat, but no bread. We had nothing to cook with but our ramrods, which we run through a piece of meat and roasted it over the fire, and to hungry soldiers it tasted sweet.*[27]

Captain John Chilton of General Mercer's old regiment, the 3rd Virginia, was also attached to General Stirling's brigade, (which was encamped along the river on Mercer's left flank) and recalled that

> *The weather was extremely cold and duty hard, when we encamped at Blue Mount* [Bowman's Hill] *the men bare of clothes and to a man we all had* [the camp itch].[28]

David Griffith, the regimental surgeon of the 3rd Virginia, did not comment on the condition of his men, but rather,

---

[27] "Personal Recollections of Captain Enoch Anderson, an Officer of the Delaware Regiment in the Revolutionary War," *Papers of the Historical Society of Delaware,* Vol. 16, (Wilmington: The Historical Society of Delaware, 1896), 28

[28] Michael Cecere, "Captain John Chilton to his brother Charles Chilton, 11 February, 1777," *The Behaved Like Soldiers*, (Bowie, MD: Heritage Books, 2004), 91

lamented the lack of support given to Washington's army by the populace:

> *We have much need for a speedy re-inforcement. I am much afraid we shall not have it in time to prevent the destruction of American affairs... Everything here wears the face of despondency...A strange consternation seems to have seized everybody in this country. A universal dissatisfaction prevails, and everybody is furnished with an excuse for declining the publick service.*[29]

General Washington also noted the universal dissatisfaction displayed by the local populace and exclaimed that if help did not arrive soon the American cause might be lost:

> *A large part of the Jerseys have given every proof of disaffection that a people can do, & this part of Pennsylvania are equally inimical; in short your imagination can scarce extend to a situation more distressing than mine -- Our only dependence now, is upon the Speedy Inlistment of a New Army, if this fails us, I think the game will be pretty well up, as from disaffection and want of spirit & fortitude, the Inhabitants instead of resistance, are offering Submission, & taking protections from Genl Howe in Jersey.*[30]

---

[29] Tyler, "David Griffith to Major Powell, 8 December, 1776," *Tyler's Quarterly,* 101

[30] Chase and Grizzard, eds., "General Washington to Lund Washington, 10-17 December, 1776," *The Papers of George Washington,* Vol. 7, 291

Washington was equally candid about the army's prospects with his brother Samuel:

> *Between you and me I think our Affairs are in a very bad way.... I have no doubt that General Howe will still make an attempt upon Philadelphia this Winter – I see nothing to oppose him in a fortnight from this time, as the term of all the Troops except those of Virginia (reduced to almost nothing) and Smallwood's Regiment from Maryland (in the same condition) will expire in that time. In a word, my dear Sir, if every nerve is not straind to recruit the New Army with all possible Expedition I think the game is pretty near up....*[31]

General Washington was so discouraged at the course of events that he instructed Lund Washington to prepare to flee Mount Vernon:

> *Matters to my view, (but this I say in confidence to you, as a friend) wear so unfavourable an aspect...that I would look forward to unfavourable Events, & prepare Accordingly in such a manner however as to give no alarm or suspicion to any one; as one step towards it, have my Papers in such a Situation as to remove at a short notice in case an Enemy's Fleet should come up the River – When they are removed let them go immediately to my Brothers in Berkeley.*[32]

---

[31] Ibid., "General Washington to Samuel Washington, 18 December, 1776," 370

[32] Ibid., "General Washington to Lund Washington, 10-17 December, 1776," 291

The stunning news of General Charles Lee's capture by the British on December 14th, near Basking Ridge, New Jersey further dampened American morale. Lee had foolishly strayed a few miles from his troops during their slow march to join Washington and was seized by a party of British dragoons that were tipped off about Lee's location by local Tories.

Dr. Benjamin Rush of Philadelphia observed the impact of Lee's capture upon Washington's troops:

> *Since the captivity of Gen Lee a distrust has crept in among the troops of the abilities of some of our general officers high in command. They expect nothing now from heaven taught & book taught Generals.*[33]

Although the growing discontentment among the troops for their officers was a concern, Dr. Rush identified two Virginia officers who he considered worthy of promotion:

> *Stevens must be made a Major General. He has genius as well as knowledge. Mercer must not be neglected. He has the confidence of the troops.*[34]

Whether General Washington still held the confidence of the troops like General Mercer did was unclear. Washington realized, however, that something had to be done quickly to stem the momentum of the enemy and restore American morale. He informed Congress that

---

[33] Paul H. Smith, ed., "Benjamin Rush to Richard Henry Lee, 21 December, 1776," *Letters of Delegates to Congress*, Vol. 5, (Washington D.C.: Library of Congress, 1979), 640

[34] Ibid.

> *We find Sir, that the Enemy are daily gathering strength from the disaffected; This strength, like a Snowball by rolling, will increase, unless some means can be devised to check effectually, the progress of the Enemy's Arms.*[35]

Washington's goal to check the enemy's progress received a big lift on the very day he wrote to Congress when General Horatio Gates and General John Sullivan arrived in camp.[36] Sullivan brought the remnants of General Lee's detachment, (about 2,000 troops) and Gates brought approximately 600 troops from Fort Ticonderoga.[37]

Another piece of good news reached camp prior to the arrival of Gates and Sullivan. Deciding, for the moment, to suspend operations against the rebels, General Howe ordered his troops into winter quarters in mid-December. Washington speculated that Howe was only waiting for the river to freeze and for the rebel army to shrink further before he resumed operations, probably in January, but the American commander welcomed the brief respite regardless.

To provide his men with adequate shelter, General Howe dispersed his British and Hessian troops among several towns in New Jersey. The overconfident British commander posted only 1,400 Hessian troops in Trenton under Colonel Johann Rall.[38] It was this force that caught General Washington's attention.

---

[35] Chase and Grizzard, eds., "General Washington to John Hancock, 20 December, 1776," *The Papers of George Washington,* Vol. 7, 381-82

[36] Ibid., 382

[37] Ibid., "General Washington to Robert Morris,22 December, 1776," 412

[38] David Hackett Fischer, *Washington's Crossing*, Appendix H, (Oxford University Press: 2004), 396

Plan to Attack Trenton Forms

General Howe's decision to disperse his troops throughout New Jersey presented General Washington with an opportunity. On December 22nd, Colonel Joseph Reed, Washington's adjutant general, informed the American commander that 600 Pennsylvania militia had recently crossed the river a few miles south of Trenton to harass the enemy.[39] Reed, who was on the western shore of the Delaware River at Bristol, urged General Washington to send additional parties across the river into New Jersey to join the harassment. He forcefully asserted in a letter to Washington that

> *We are all of Opinion my dear General that something must be attempted to revive our expiring Credit, give our Cause some Degree of Reputation & prevent a total Depreciation of the Continental Money which is coming on Very fast – that even a Failure cannot be more fatal than to remain in our present Situation. In short some Enterprize must be undertaken in our present Circumstances or we must give up the Cause.*[40]

Reed acknowledged the imminent departure of more than half of Washington's army at the end of December and urged the American commander to act decisively against the enemy while he still could:

---

[39] Chase and Grizzard, eds., "From Colonel Joseph Reed, 22 December, 1776," *The Papers of George Washington,* Vol. 7, 415

[40] Ibid.

> *In a little Time the Continental Army* [will be] *dissolved. The Militia must be* [used] *before their Spirits & Patience are exhausted & the scattered, divided State of the Enemy affords us a fair Oppy...* [to see] *what our Men will do when called to an offensive Attack – Will it not be possible my dear Genl for your Troops...to make a Diversion or something more at or about Trenton?*[42]

Reed continued:

> *I will not disguise my own Sentiments that our Cause is desperate & hopeless if we do not take the Oppy of the Collection of Troops at present to strike some Stroke. Our Affairs are* [hastening] *fast to Ruin if we do not retrieve them by some happy Event. Delay with us is now equal to a total Defeat.*[43]

Washington received Reed's letter in the afternoon of December 22nd and held a council of war that evening. General Mercer and Washington's other brigade commanders shared their thoughts on an attack on Trenton and although no record of the war council exists to inform us what was said, General Washington revealed the outcome of the meeting to Colonel Reed the next day:

> *Christmas day at Night, one hour before day is the time fixed upon for our Attempt on Trenton. For heaven's sake keep this to yourself, as the discovery of it may prove fatal to us, our numbers, sorry I am to*

---

[42] Ibid.
[43] Ibid.

> *say, being less than I had any conception of – but necessity, dire necessity will – nay must justify any* [*attempt*].[44]

The next day, Christmas Eve, General Washington held another war council at General Greene's headquarters (the home of Samuel Merrick) to finalize his plan of attack.[45] The objective was Colonel Johann Rall's 1,400 man Hessian garrison at Trenton. The operation against the Hessians would involve over 5,000 troops in three simultaneous night crossings of the Delaware River along a twenty mile front.

Recently promoted General John Cadwalader, with approximately 1,000 Pennsylvania militia and 850 newly arrived New England continentals was ordered to cross the river ten miles south of Trenton to engage the enemy around Burlington and Bordentown and prevent their relief of Trenton.[46] General James Ewing, with approximately 1,100 militia from Pennsylvania and New Jersey was ordered to cross the river at Trenton Ferry (just south of Trenton) to prevent the Hessian garrison at Trenton from fleeing southward once General Washington attacked the town from the north.[47]

Washington planned to cross the river about nine miles above Trenton with the troops he had led into Pennsylvania earlier in the month and the recently arrived troops of General Sullivan (formerly Lee) and General Gates. Leaving the

---

[44] Ibid., "General Washington to Colonel Joseph Reed, 23 December, 1776," 423

[45] William S. Stryker, *The Battles of Trenton and Princeton*, (Old Barracks Association, 2001), 113
Originally published in 1898

[46] Ibid., 344-46

[47] Ibid. 346-47

infirm and a baggage guard behind in camp, Washington's force numbered approximately 2,400 men. They were divided into two divisions under General Sullivan and General Greene. Mercer's brigade was attached to Greene's division.

Washington's men did not realize it as they slept along the west bank of the Delaware River that Christmas Eve, but the fate of the American rebellion rested on their shoulders.

Battle of Trenton

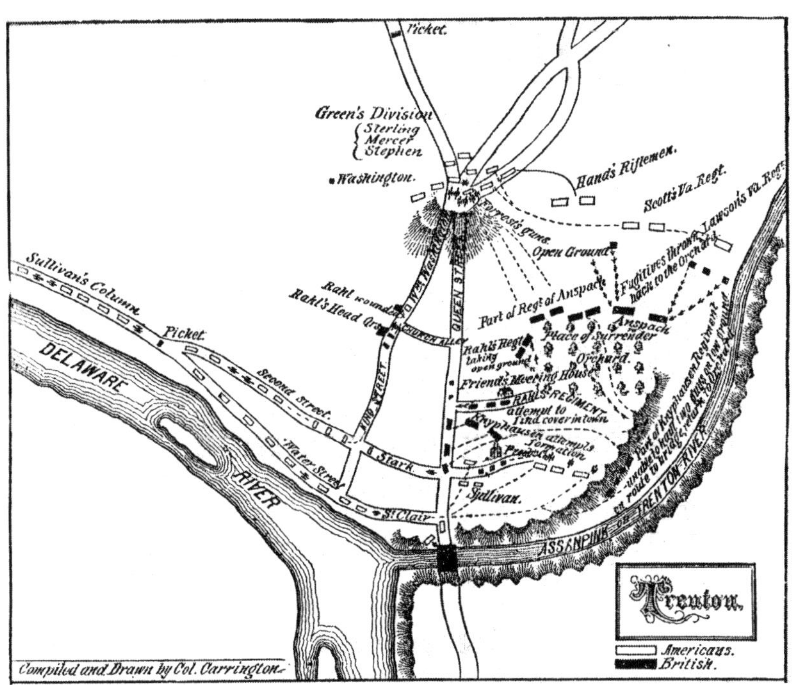

Chapter Six

"Charge Bayonets and Rush On!"

Battle of Trenton

December 1776

General Mercer and his troops awoke on Christmas day to frigid temperatures in the teens.[1] Ice had formed along the shoreline of the Delaware River and large pieces of floe ice floated downriver, swept along by a swift current. Such conditions promised a difficult time crossing the river.

Posted in the vicinity of McKonkey's Ferry, General Mercer's brigade had entered its third week along the banks of the Delaware. Three days earlier, over 800 officers and men had reported for duty, and although this was a far cry from full strength for his brigade, it was about average for all of the brigades in Washington's army.[2]

The troops in Mercer's brigade hailed from Connecticut, Massachusetts, Maryland, and Virginia, and the last few months had been hard on them. Most were planning to leave the army and return to their homes in a week when their enlistments expired on December 31st. They were a bit surprised and concerned, therefore, when General Mercer issued the following orders to his regimental commanders on Christmas Day:

---

[1] Fischer, "Appendix K : Weather Records in the Delaware Valley, 1776-77," *Washington's Crossing*, 401

[2] Force, ed., "Return of the Forces in the Service of the States of America...under the Command of General Washington... 22 December, 1776," *American Archives*, Fifth Series, Vol. 3, 1401

> *You are to see that your men have three days provisions ready cooked before 12 o' clock this forenoon – the whole fit for duty except a Serjeant and six men to be left with the baggage, and to parade precisely at four in the afternoon with their arms, accoutrements & ammunition in the best order, with their provisions and blankets – you will have them told off in divisions in which order they are to march – eight men a breast, with the officers fixed to their divisions from which they are on no account to separate – no man is to quit his division on pain of instant punishment – each officer is to provide himself with a piece of white paper stuck in his hat for a field mark. You will order your men to assemble and parade them in the valley immediately over the hill on the back of McConkey's Ferry, to remain there for farther orders – a profound silence is to be observed, both by officers and men, and a strict and ready attention paid to whatever orders may be given....*[3]

General Mercer's brigade marched to McKonkey's Ferry in the fading light of Christmas Day; his was the second brigade, behind General Stephen's Virginians, to cross the river. The wind had picked up considerably and the thickening clouds signaled the approach of a storm. While they waited on the Jersey shore for the rest of Washington's army to cross the river, Mercer's men huddled around large bonfires to stay warm, unaware of what was in store for them.

---

[3] Stryker, "General Mercer to Colonel Durkee, 25 December, 1776," *The Battles of Trenton and Princeton*, 379

Challenged by a swift current and deteriorating weather conditions, the river crossing fell behind schedule. Snow and freezing rain began to fall around 11 p.m. and a brisk wind made the night miserable for all who were exposed to it.[4] John Greenwood, a young fifer from Massachusetts in Colonel John Paterson's 15th Continental Regiment (Sullivan's Division) recalled that, "*it rained, hailed, snowed and froze, and at the same time blew a perfect hurricane*."[5] Like General Mercer's troops, Greenwood struggled to stay warm around a large bonfire while he waited on the Jersey side of the river for the rest of the army and equipment to cross. He remembered that

> *When I turned my face towards the fire my back would be freezing.... By turning round and round I kept myself from perishing....*[6]

General Washington had crossed with Stephen's brigade (the first to cross) and waited impatiently near the shoreline for the rest of the army. Wrapped in a cloak, the American commander rested on a wooden box and grew increasingly concerned that as they fell behind schedule, the element of surprise slipping away.[7] Washington explained to Congress that as the night wore on

---

[4] Stryker, 133

[5] Isaac J. Greenwood, ed., *The Revolutionary Services of John Greenwood*... 1775-1783, (New York, 1922), 39

[6] Ibid.

[7] Fischer, 219

> [I began to] *Despair of surprising the Town, as I well knew we could not reach* [Trenton] *before the day was fairly broke, but as I was certain there was no making a Retreat without being discovered, and harassed on repassing the River, I determined to push on at all Events.*[8]

The two other American detachments downriver from Trenton that were involved in the attack faced equally difficult conditions. Stymied by poor weather and growing ice, General Cadwalader and General Ewing suspended their assaults after struggling for hours to cross the river. Both assumed that General Washington had met a similar fate.

Washington, unaware of developments to the south, carried on. Colonel Henry Knox of Massachusetts actively supervised the crossing at McKonkey's Ferry and did all he could to expedite the process. Major James Wilkinson acknowledged Knox's efforts:

> *The force of the current, the sharpness of the frost, the darkness of the night, the ice…and high wind, rendered the passage of the river extremely difficult; and but for the stentorian lungs and extraordinary exertions of Colonel Knox it could not have been* [accomplished in time] *to favour the enterprize.* [9]

---

[8] Chase and Grizzard, eds., "General Washington to John Hancock, 27 December, 1776," *The Papers of George Washington,* Vol. 7, 454

[9] James Wilkinson, *Memoirs of My Own Times*, Vol. 1, (Philadelphia: Abraham Small, 1816), 128

March to Trenton

The last of Washington's eighteen cannon were unloaded on the Jersey shore sometime after 3 a.m. and the half frozen American troops began a nine mile march to Trenton in one long column. John Greenwood, a soldier in General Sullivan's division, recalled that

> *We began an apparently circuitous march, not advancing faster than a child ten years old could walk, and stopping frequently.... During the whole night it alternately hailed, rained, snowed, and blew tremendously... At one time, when we halted on the road, I sat on a stump of a tree and was so benumbed with cold that I wanted to go to sleep; had I been passed unnoticed I should have frozen to death...but as good luck always attended me, Sergeant Madden came and, rousing me up, made me walk about.*[10]

Major James Wilkinson, who was also attached to Sullivan's division, had observed earlier in the day that the march route to McKonkey's Ferry, "*was easily traced, as there was a little snow on the ground, which was tinged here and there with blood from the feet of the men who wore broken shoes*."[11] This undoubtedly continued to be the case during the long, difficult march to Trenton. In fact, private Greenwood recalled that

---

[10] Greenwood, ed., *The Revolutionary Services of John Greenwood...* 1775-1783, 39

[11] Wilkinson, 127

> *We were...nearly half dead with cold for the want of clothing, as, putting the storm to one side, many of our soldiers had not a shoe to their feet and their clothes were ragged as those of a begger.*[12]

Despite the hardship and fatigue of the march, Colonel Knox recalled that, "*the troops marched with the most profound silence and in good order.*"[13] They were urged on by General Washington himself, who rode up and down the column imploring the troops to, "*Keep by your officers, for Gods Sake keep by your officers.*"[14]

About half way to Trenton Washington's column split. General Sullivan led his division along the River Road to strike Trenton from the west while General Greene led his division (which included Mercer's brigade) along the Pennington Road to strike Trenton from the north.

Battle of Trenton

As dawn broke, Washington's troops were still several miles from town and the element of surprise was in doubt. Fortunately, the same fierce storm that delayed Washington's march caused the Hessians to let down their guard. Morning patrols that would have normally discovered the approaching

---

[12] Greenwood, ed., *The Revolutionary Services of John Greenwood...* 1775-1783, 39

[13] Francis Drake, ed., *The Life and Correspondence of Henry Knox*, (Boston, 1873), 36

[14] William S. Powell, ed., "A Connecticut Soldier Under Washington: Elisha Bostwick's Memoirs of the First Years of the Revolution," *The William and Mary Quarterly,* 3rd Series, Vol. 6, No. 1 (Jan. 1949), 102

Americans were cut short due to the bad weather.[15] The Hessian piquets did not discover Washington's advance until the Americans were upon them. The commander of one Hessian piquet post, Lieutenant Andreas Wiederhold, recalled that

> *If I had not just stepped out of my little guard-house and seen the enemy, they might have been upon me before I had time to reach for my rifle, as my sentinels did not keep a very sharp lookout any more as it was broad daylight....*[16]

It was 8:00 a.m. and the Americans had largely achieved the surprise they so desperately sought. General Greene's division had approached to within 800 yards of the Hessian outposts and had deployed for battle, going from a long column into a battle line.[17] General Mercer's brigade formed on the right, Stephen's (with Stirling's Delaware Regiment) was in the center and Fermoy's brigade deployed to the left of Stephen.[18] General Stirling followed with the rest of his brigade in reserve. The entire division swept along both sides of the Pennington Road at a trot and overwhelmed the Hessian piquets.[19] To the west, General Sullivan's division launched a nearly simultaneous attack.

Washington's troops quickly pushed the Hessian picquets towards Trenton and followed them, "*pell-mell*" into town.[20]

---

[15] Chase and Grizzard, eds., Excerpt of Lt. Andreas Wiederhold's Diary, Note 7, *The Papers of George Washington,* Vol. 7, 457-58
[16] Ibid.
[17] Fischer, 235
[18] Ibid.
[19] Ibid.
[20] Drake, ed., *The Life and Correspondence of Henry Knox*, 36

The startled Hessians attempted to form in the streets but were peppered by American artillery fire. Colonel Knox described the effect of American cannon fire on the Hessians:

> *The hurry, fright, and confusion of the enemy was (not) unlike that which will be when the last trumpet shall sound. They endeavoured to form in streets, the heads of which we had previously the possession of with cannon and howitzers; these, in a twinkling of an eye, cleared the streets. The backs of the houses were resorted to for shelter. These proved ineffectual:* [our] *musketry soon dislodged them.*[21]

According to John Greenwood, who was with General Sullivan's division on the River Road, it was not American musketry that dislodged the enemy but sheer numbers:

> *As we had been in the storm all night we were not only wet through and through ourselves, but our guns and powder were wet also, so that I do not believe one would go off and I saw none fired by our party.... We advanced, and although there was not more than one bayonet to five men, orders were given to, 'Charge bayonets and rush on!' and rush on we did. Within pistol-shot they again fired point-blank at us; we dodged and they did not hit a man, while before they had time to reload we were within three feet of them, when they broke in an instant and ran like so many frightened devils into town, which was a short distance, we after them pell-mell.*[22]

---

[21] Ibid.

[22] Greenwood, ed., *The Revolutionary Services of John Greenwood...* 1775-1783, 41

Major Wilkinson credited American artillery fire, which swept Trenton with canister and grape shot, with dispersing the enemy:

> *The enemy made a momentary shew of resistance by a wild and undirected fire from the windows of their quarters which they abandoned as we advanced, and made an attempt to form in the main street, which might have succeeded but for a six gun battery opened by Captain T. Forest...at the head of King's Street, which annoyed the enemy in various directions.*[23]

The Hessian commander, Colonel Johann Rall, rallied his men in an orchard east of town and attempted to attack Washington's left flank near the Princeton Road, but General Washington acted quickly and shifted more troops to that position to secure it.[24]

With large numbers of hostile troops on his front and flanks, Colonel Rall's next move should have been an attempted retreat across the Assunpink Creek. Instead, the proud Hessian commander ordered his men back into town to recapture two abandoned cannon.[25] The outnumbered Hessians bravely marched back towards the center of Trenton and were pummeled with musket and cannon fire from three directions. To their front was General Mercer's brigade, many of who had found shelter in houses and outbuilding which allowed them to dry their muskets.[26] Mercer's men

---

[23] Wilkinson, 129
[24] Fischer, 246
[25] Ibid.
[26] Ibid.

discharged deadly shots into the advancing Hessians, who were also assailed on their flanks by the infantry of General Greene's and General Sullivan's divisions. Heavy cannon fire from Colonel Knox's guns at the head of King Street also took a toll, and yet, a party of Hessians reached their abandoned guns.

It was at this moment that one of General Mercer's former officers in the 3rd Virginia Regiment, Captain William Washington, leapt into action. Major James Wilkinson recounted that

> *Captain Washington, who, seconded by Lieutenant James Monroe, led the advanced guard of the left column, perceiving that the enemy were endeavouring to form a battery, rushed forward, drove the artillerists from their guns, and took two pieces in the act of firing.*[27]

Joseph White, a New England artillerist who joined Captain Washington's assault with a detachment of artillerymen recalled that

> *I hallowed as loud as I could scream to the men to run for their lives right up to the* [cannon]. *I was the first that reach them.* [The Hessians] *had all left except one man tending the vent.*[28]

White frightened the remaining Hessian away and then he and his men turned the captured guns on the enemy. "*We put in a canister of shot (they had put in a cartridge before they left it)*

---

[27] Wilkinson, 130
[28] Fischer, 247

and fired," recalled Sergeant White.[29] Captain Washington and Lieutenant Monroe were both seriously wounded in the charge, but the Hessian guns were secured and the battle approached its dramatic conclusion.

The loss of their cannon, as well as their commander, Colonel Rall, (who was mortally wounded upon his horse) dispirited the Hessians. They withdrew back to the orchard, closely pursued by the Americans who pressed them on three sides. Trapped by the Assunpink Creek in their rear, and the Americans on their front and flanks, the Hessians had little choice but to surrender. They had suffered over one hundred casualties in the battle while the Americans lost just a handful of men.[30] General Washington's attack on Trenton was a staggering success for the Americans, garnering over 900 Hessian prisoners along with much needed supplies.[31] More importantly, the victory provided a huge boost to American morale.

The threat of a British counterattack from Princeton prompted Washington to immediately march his weary army back to McKonkey's Ferry to re-cross the river. His exhausted troops literally collapsed in camp upon their return in the evening, but they rested with a strong sense of accomplishment; their victory at Trenton restored hope in the American cause.

---

[29] Ibid.
[30] Stryker, 196, 194
[31] Ibid. 386

Trenton and Vicinity

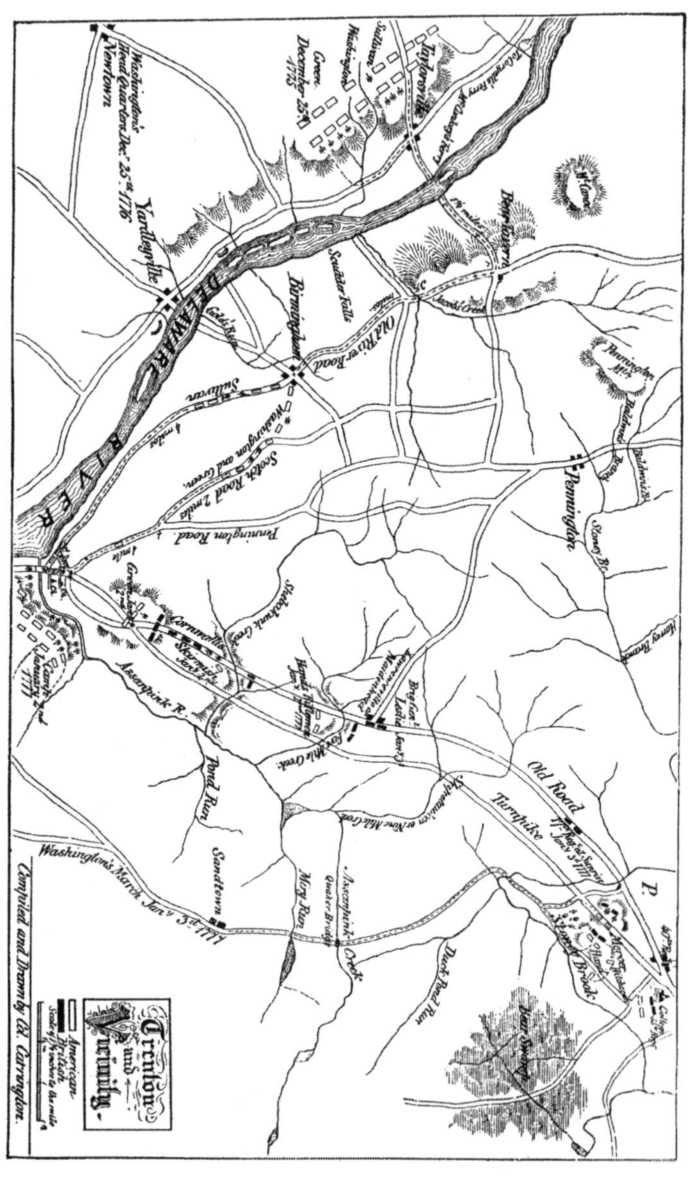

Chapter Seven

"Cheer Up My Boys, the Day is Ours!"

Battle of Princeton : January 1777

General Washington wished to capitalize on his success at Trenton and called a council of war on the evening of December 27th, to determine how to proceed. Unaware that his surprising victory at Trenton had caused the enemy to abandon their outposts in western New Jersey, General Washington hinted to one officer the course he hoped to follow.

> *If we could happily beat up the rest of their quarters bordering on & near the River it would be attended with the most valuable consequences.*[1]

Washington mistakenly believed that General Cadwalader, with 1,500 Pennsylvania militia, was encamped downriver a few miles ready to join Washington on a new expedition. Prior to the war council, however, Washington was surprised to learn that Cadwalader was already across the Delaware River in New Jersey.

Upon news of the American victory at Trenton, General Cadwalader, who had abandoned his own crossing on Christmas night, crossed the river into New Jersey near

---

[1] Chase and Grizzard, eds., "General Washington to Colonel Cadwalader, 27 December, 1776," *The Papers of George Washington,* Vol. 7, 450

Bristol; he assumed that Washington was still in Trenton. Surprised to learn that General Washington had returned to Pennsylvania on the same day of the attack, Cadwalader decided to stay in New Jersey and reported to Washington that the enemy had abandoned their outposts and was nowhere to be found.[2] Cadwalader added that

> *If you should think proper to cross over, it may be easily effected at the place where we passed – A pursuit would keep up the Panic – They went off with great precipitation, & press'd all the Waggons in their reach – I am told many of them are gone to South Amboy – If we can drive them from West Jersey, the Success will raise an Army by next Spring, & establish the Credit of the Continental Money, to support it.*[3]

General Cadwalader's call for offensive action was repeated by Washington's adjutant general, Colonel Joseph Reed. He had crossed into New Jersey with Cadwalader and had advanced with a small party of horsemen as far as Trenton, which he found abandoned by the enemy. Colonel Reed sent a dispatch to Washington and urged him to, "*cross the River again & pursue the Advantages which Providence had presented....*"[4] It was this proposal, to re-cross the Delaware River, that dominated the discussion of Washington's war council on December 27th.

---

[2] Ibid., "Colonel Cadwalader to General Washington, 27 December, 1776," 451-52

[3] Ibid.

[4] Joseph Reed, "General Joseph Reed's Narrative of the Movements of the American Army in the Neighborhood of Trenton in the Winter of 1776-77," *Pennsylvania Magazine of History and Biography*, Vol. 8, (1884), 397

Unfortunately, no record of the council's proceedings exists, but Colonel Reed, who presumably learned what was discussed from some of the participants, reported that

> *Some Doubts, it is said, arose in the General Council on this Occasion some of the Members who disapproved the Enterprize advised sending Orders to the Militia to return, but the General & some others declared that tho' they would not have advised* [Cadwalader's] *Movement yet being done it ought to be supported & the Orders were accordingly issued for the Troops to prepare to cross the River.*[5]

Washington allowed his troops another day to, "*recover from their late fatigue*," before he ordered them to cross the Delaware on December 29th.[6] General Mercer's brigade crossed with Greene's division at Yardley's Ferry. Lieutenant James McMichael, who was attached to General Greene's division, described his return to New Jersey in his diary:

> *Having again received marching orders, we got ready at dark, and at 10 P.M. crossed at Yardley, where we lodged. Weather very cold, snow 6 inches deep, no tents, and no houses to lodge in*![7]

Washington's army entered Trenton the next day and encamped upon rising ground on the east side of the Assunpink Creek, just outside of town. Cannon guarded the single bridge that spanned the creek and General Mercer, along with Colonel John Glover of Massachusetts, was

---

[5] Ibid.

[6] Chase and Grizzard, eds., "General Washington to General Heath, 28 December, 1776," *The Papers of George Washington,* Vol. 7, 468

[7] McMichael, 140

ordered to form several guard details from among their brigades to patrol the roads into Trenton.[8]

Washington Appeals to the Troops

While Washington's troops settled into Trenton, the American commander and his officers addressed an impending crisis. More than half of the continental troops in the army, including the bulk of General Mercer's brigade, were due to be discharged on January 1st. General Washington resolved to appeal to the troops himself to stay a month longer and addressed the men on December 30th. A sergeant in General Mercer's brigade provided a vivid description of what occurred:

> *At this trying time General Washington, having now but a little handful of men and many of them new recruits in which he could place but little confidence, ordered our regiment to be paraded, and personally addressed us, urging that we should stay a month longer. He alluded to our recent victory at Trenton; told us that our services were greatly needed, and that we could now do more for our country than we ever could at any future period; and in the most affectionate manner entreated us to stay. The drums beat for volunteers, but not a man turned out. The soldiers worn down with fatigue and privations, had their hearts fixed on home and the comforts of the domestic circle, and it was hard to forego the anticipated pleasures of the society of our dearest friends.*[9]

---

[8] Ibid., "General Orders, 30 December, 1776," 484

[9] Sergeant R, "The Battle of Princeton," *Pennsylvania Magazine of History and Biography,* Vol. 20, No. 4 (1896), 515-16

General Washington was dismayed at the reaction of the men and tried one more time to convince them to stay:

> *The General wheeled his horse about, rode in front of the regiment, and addressing us again said, 'My brave fellows, you have done all I asked you to do, and more than could be reasonably expected; but your country is at stake, your wives, your houses, and all that you hold dear. You have worn yourselves out with fatigues and hardships, but we know not how to spare you. If you will consent to stay only one month longer, you will render that service to the cause of liberty, and to your country, which you probably never can do under any other circumstances. The present is emphatically the crisis, which is to decide out destiny.'*
>
> *The drums beat the second time. The soldiers felt the force of the appeal. One said to another, 'I will remain if you will.' Others remarked 'We cannot go home under such circumstanced.' A few stepped forth, and their example was immediately followed by nearly all who were fit for duty in the regiment, amounting to about two hundred volunteers. An officer enquired of the General if these men should be enrolled. He replied, --'No! men who will volunteer in such a case as this, need no enrollment to keep them to their duty.*[10]

Although Washington's appeal did not convince all of the troops to stay, approximately half accepted the $10 bounty and agreed to remain in the ranks for another month. The core of

---

[10] Ibid.

Washington's army, his veteran continentals, was weaken, but still intact.

The departure of hundreds of troops on January 1st, combined with a serious illness for General Stirling, resulted in the temporary merging of Stirling's and Mercer's brigades under the command of General Mercer. This arrangement reunited Mercer with the remnants of his old command, the 3rd Virginia Regiment. A large portion of the regiment, which had shrunk to less than 150 effective men, had been detached to escort the Hessian prisoners from Trenton to Philadelphia, but it appears that at least a portion of the 3rd Virginia was with the brigade in Trenton by the start of the new year.[11] Colonel George Weedon, Mercer's brother-in-law, was unfortunately not one of them. He went to Philadelphia with the guard detail.

General Stirling's depleted brigade of the 1st and 3rd Virginia Regiments, the 1st Delaware Regiment, and the 1st Pennsylvania Rifle Regiment, did not offset the troop losses Mercer's own brigade suffered at the departure of many of his New England continentals, but it did bring General Mercer's troop strength to nearly 400 men fit for duty.[12] Initially, General Washington expected Mercer's troops, along with General Stephen's Virginian continentals, to form the first of three infantry lines behind the artillery should the enemy

---

[11] Michael Cecere, "Diary of Captain John Chilton, 3 January, 1777," *They Behaved Like Soldiers: Captain John Chilton and the 3rd Virginia Regiment,* (Bowie, MD: Heritage Books, 2004), 114

[12] Robert Selig, Matthew Harris, and Wade P. Catts, *Battle of Princeton Mapping Project: Report of Military Terrain Analysis and Battle Narrative, Princeton, New Jersey,* (September, 2010), 46

advance on Trenton, but these defensive arrangements were soon adjusted.[13]

While Washington settled into Trenton and considered his next move, General Mercer had occasion to dine with General Arthur St. Clair's at St. Clair's quarters. General St. Clair was a fellow Scotsman who had studied medicine in Edinburgh before joining the British army and serving in America in the French and Indian War.[14] St. Clair resigned his officer's commission in 1762 and settled in western Pennsylvania where he became a prominent landowner.[15] He commanded a Pennsylvania regiment against the British in Canada in 1776 and was promoted to brigadier-general in August. St. Clair joined Washington's army just prior to the Battle of Trenton as part of the force commanded by General Gates and led a brigade of New Hampshire and Massachusetts troops at the Battle of Trenton.[16] By the start of 1777, General St. Clair commanded the remnants of a dozen New England regiments (those who had agreed to remain an extra month).[17]

Dr. Benjamin Rush (who had just arrived from the Pennsylvania militia camp of General Cadwalader at Crosswicks) joined General Mercer and General St. Clair for dinner in Trenton and recalled years later in his memoirs that

---

[13] Chase and Grizzard, eds., "General Orders, 30 December, 1776," *The Papers of George Washington,* Vol. 7, 484

[14] Mark Mayo Boatner III, *Encyclopedia of the American Revolution,* (NY: David McKay Co., 1966), 956

[15] Ibid.

[16] Stryker, 354

[17] Fischer, 408

> *The two Generals* [Mercer and St. Clair] *both Scotchmen, and men of highly cultivated minds, poured forth strains of noble sentiments in their conversation. General Mercer said 'he would not be conquered, but that he would cross the mountains and live among the Indians rather than submit to the power of Great Britain in any of the civilized States.'*[18]

Major James Wilkinson also recalled an exchange with General Mercer at General St. Clair's quarters on January 1st. It was later in the evening and Major Wilkinson, exhausted by the day's activities, had lain down in St. Clair's quarters to rest when he overheard General Mercer express his disapproval at the promotion of Captain William Washington of the 3rd Virginia Regiment to the rank of Major of a troop of cavalry.[19] The other officers confessed their surprise at Mercer's position, especially given that Captain Washington had received the promotion for gallantry at the Battle of Trenton. Mercer explained his position by declaring that

> *We are not engaged in a war of ambition; if it had been so, I should have never have accepted a commission under a man who had not seen a day's service (alluding to the great orator, and distinguished patriot, Patrick Henry) we serve not for ourselves but for our country, and every man should be content to fill the place in which he can be most useful.*[20]

---

[18] Benjamin Rush, *A Memorial Containing Travels Through Life or Sundry Incidents in the Life of Dr. Benjamin Rush,* (Louis Alexander Biddle, 1905), 95

[19] Wilkinson, 146

[20] Ibid.

General Mercer admitted that Captain Washington was a good infantry commander, but he insisted that that did not mean Washington was destined to be a good cavalry officer. "*I have seen good captains make indifferent majors*," announced Mercer, and he ended with a bold declaration:

> *My views in this contest are confined to a single object, that is, the success of the cause, and God can witness how cheerfully I would lay down my life to secure it.*[21]

General Mercer's declaration would soon be put to the test.

Council of War

General Mercer and the other officers who attended Washington's war council on January 1st, had several issues to consider. The latest intelligence reported that 7,000 to 8,000 enemy troops under General Cornwallis were preparing to march from Princeton to confront Washington in Trenton.[22] American forces in New Jersey surpassed 5,000 troops, but they were scattered about western New Jersey in several detachments. Washington commanded approximately 1,600 continentals (fit for duty) at Trenton, General Cadwalader commanded 1,800 militia at Crosswicks (eight miles from Trenton) while General Thomas Mifflin commanded another 1,800 militia at Bordentown (about seven miles from Trenton).[23]

---

[21] Ibid.

[22] Joseph Reed, "General Joseph Reed's Narrative of the Movements of the American Army in the Neighborhood of Trenton in the Winter of 1776-77," *Pennsylvania Magazine of History and Biography*, Vol. 8, 400

[23] Chase and Grizzard, eds., "General Washington to John Hancock, 1 January, 1777," *The Papers of George Washington,* Vol. 7, 504-505

There was disagreement among Washington's officers at the war council on what to do. Some argued that Washington should leave Trenton and march to either Crosswicks or Bordentown to unite with the militia, others argued that the militia should march to Trenton to unite with Washington. A few officers proposed that General Cadwalader strike New Brunswick (which was assumed to be weakened by the transfer of British troops to Princeton) while Washington remained in Trenton and reacted to the situation. Others suggested that all of the American forces withdraw across the Delaware River immediately.[24]

It is impossible to tell what advice General Mercer offered, but at the end of the council General Washington made the decision to concentrate all of his troops in Trenton. Washington explained his decision to Congress:

> *Our situation was most critical and our force small. To remove immediately was again destroying every dawn of hope which had begun to revive in the breasts of the Jersey Militia, and to bring those Troops which had first crossed the Delaware, and were laying at Croswix's under Genl Cadwalader & those under Genl Mifflin at Bordenton (amounting in the whole to about 3600) to Trenton, was to bring them to an exposed place; One or the other however was unavoidable, the latter was preferred & they were ordered to join us at Trenton....*[25]

---

[24] Joseph Reed, "General Joseph Reed's Narrative of the Movements of the American Army in the Neighborhood of Trenton in the Winter of 1776-77," *Pennsylvania Magazine of History and Biography*, Vol. 8, 400

[25] Chase and Grizzard, eds., "General Washington to John Hancock, 5 January, 1777," *The Papers of George Washington,* Vol. 7, 520-521

Washington issued orders to General Cadwalader and General Mifflin that same night to march their militia with all possible speed to Trenton.[26] They arrived early on January 2nd. Ten miles to the northeast in Princeton, General Charles Cornwallis and nearly eight thousand British and Hessian soldiers, eager to avenge their loss at Trenton, marched westward to engage General Washington.[27]

Second Battle of Trenton

General Washington, aware of the approaching danger, deployed the bulk of his troops along a two mile front behind the Assunpink Creek. This deep creek presented a strong obstacle to a British assault. Washington's left flank was secured by the Delaware River but his right flank "hung in the air" and was thus vulnerable. It was crucial that whoever defended the American right flank hold firm else the enemy might force the Americans back to the river and pin them there. General Washington gave the responsibility of defending the right flank to General Mercer and his 400 men.[28]

To give his army some warning of the enemy's approach and slow their advance to Trenton, General Washington deployed a detachment of approximately 1,000 troops under General Fermoy a few miles up the Princeton Road.[29] It was these troops that first confronted the British army on their march to Trenton.

---

[26] Ibid., "General Washington to Colonel John Cadwalader or Brigadier General Thomas Mifflin, 1 January, 1777," 510

[27] Fischer, 291

[28] Stryker, 263

[29] Fischer, 281

General Cornwallis and his men struggled westward on January 2nd, through a quagmire of mud churned up by thousands of men, horses and wagons. As they approached the position of the American advance guard along Shabbakonk Creek, the American commander, General Fermoy, suddenly mounted his horse and rode off towards Trenton.[30]

Luckily for the Americans, Fermoy's second in command, Colonel Edward Hand of Pennsylvania, an experienced officer who had served in the siege of Boston in 1775 and in many of the battles around New York in 1776, assumed command. With his men hidden deep in the woods along the creek, Colonel Hand instructed them to hold their fire until the British troops were almost on top of them, at which point Hand's men unleashed a devastating fire followed by a charge that drove Cornwallis's lead element back onto his main body.[31] Major James Wilkinson, who learned about the engagement from a participant, claimed in his memoirs that

> *The boldness of this manoeuver menacing a general attack, induced the enemy to form in order of battle and bring up his artillery and open a battery, with which he scoured the wood for half an hour before he entered it.*[32]

Colonel Hand's men were eventually forced to withdraw westward and reform on the outskirts of Trenton. General Washington arrived and urged the American skirmishers to delay Cornwallis until nightfall. A thirty-minute artillery duel slowed the British, but they eventually overwhelmed the

---

[30] Stryker, 259
[31] Wilkinson, 137
[32] Ibid.

Americans and pushed into town. Washington's advance troops raced to the Assunpink Bridge to make one last stand. With over an hour of daylight left for Cornwallis to strike and perhaps defeat Washington's army, the Americans found themselves in a grave situation. Virginian Robert Beale was posted at the bridge and recalled:

> *This was a most awful crisis. No possible chance of crossing the* [Delaware] *river; ice as large as houses floating down, and no retreat to the mountains, the British between us and them. Our brigade, consisting of the Fourth, Fifth, and Sixth Virginia Regiments, was ordered to form in column at the bridge and General Washington came and, in the presence of us all, told Colonel Scott to defend the bridge to the last extremity. Colonel Scott answered with an oath, 'Yes, General, as long as there is a man alive.'*[33]

Major James Wilkinson also noted the urgency of the situation:

> *If ever there was a crisis in the affairs of the revolution, this was the moment; thirty minutes would have sufficed to bring the two armies into contact, and thirty more would have decided the combat....*[34]

---

[33] Dennis P. Ryan, "Robert Beale Memoirs," *A Salute to Courage: The American Revolution as Seen Through Wartime Writings of Officers of the Continental Army and Navy*, (NY: Columbia University Press, 1979), 56

[34] Wilkinson, 138

British and Hessian troops mounted three assaults against the bridge, but each charge was repulsed by a barrage of American small arms and artillery fire. The Americans would not budge, and with the last rays of daylight fading in the west, General Cornwallis suspended his attack until morning. The American advance troops had bought Washington's army a twelve hour reprieve, and the American commander-in-chief made full use of it.

March to Princeton

General Washington convened yet another war council with his brigade commanders after dark to discuss their next move. Major James Wilkinson, who served as an aide to General St. Clair, did not attend the council but learned of its proceedings from St. Clair and described the meeting years later in his memoirs:

> *General Washington...had but a brief statement to submit to his council; the situation of the two armies were known to all; a battle was certain if he kept his ground until the morning, and in case of an action a defeat was to be apprehended.* [35]

Wilkinson remembered that some in the council suggested a retreat downriver to avoid an engagement while others, including General Washington, leaned towards making a stand along the Assunpink.[36] Then General St. Clair proposed a third option, which he recounted years later:

---

[35] Ibid., 140
[36] Ibid.

> *I had the good fortune to suggest the idea of turning the left of the enemy in the night; gaining a march upon him, and proceeding with all possible expedition to Brunswick.* [37]

General St. Clair's bold proposal was immediately endorsed by General Mercer. St. Clair remembered that

> *General Mercer immediately fell in with it, and very forcibly pointed out both its practicability, and the advantages that would necessarily result from it, and general Washington highly approved it; nor was there one dissenting voice in the council….* [38]

Lieutenant John Armstrong, an aide-de-camp to General Mercer, remembered the war council a bit differently. He credited General Mercer with proposing the move to Princeton:

> *During the evening a Council was held at Mercer's quarters (Richard's Tavern) by which the following questions were discussed – Shall a battle be risked in our present position and if not on what point a retreat be made? The first question was rejected unanimously with the qualification – Unless it be found that we cannot do better. – Such, after a good deal of discussion appeared to become the general opinion – when Mercer remarked – that one course not yet*

---

[37] Selig, Harris, and Catts, *Battle of Princeton Mapping Project: Report of Military Terrain Analysis and Battle Narrative, Princeton, New Jersey,* Appendix I, Item 120, William Henry Smith, *The St. Clair Papers: The Life and Public Services of Arthur St. Clair,* Vol. 1, 36-44

[38] Ibid.

> *suggested might be usefully explored and this was to order up the Philadelphia Militia, make a night march to Princeton – attack the two British regiments said to be there under Leclay (?) & continue our march to Brunswick....It was at this moment that Sinclair* [General St. Clair] *gave a full and clear description of the hilly region between Brunswick and Morristown – upon which the night march as suggested by Mercer was adopted and executed....*[39]

Thus, according to Lieutenant Armstrong, it was General Mercer who proposed the night march and attack on Princeton. Whether this was so is unclear, but it is clear that General Mercer, along with General St. Clair, played a significant role in reaching the decision to march to Princeton.

With agreement reached, General Washington issued orders to prepare to march. Major Wilkinson recalled that Washington

> *Ordered the guards to be doubled, a strong fatigue party to be set to work on an entrenchment across the road near the mill, within distinct hearing of the sentinels of the enemy, the baggage to be sent to Burlington, the troops to be silently filed off by detachments, and the neighbouring fences to be used*

---

[39] Selig, Harris, and Catts, *Battle of Princeton Mapping Project: Report of Military Terrain Analysis and Battle Narrative, Princeton, New Jersey,* Appendix I, Item 7, Undated "Memorandum of Gen. H. Mercer's ... services and character" by Lieutenant John Armstrong, enclosed in a letter to William B. Reed (1806-1876) of Philadelphia dated 13 September 1839, in response to an inquiry of 8 July 1839 concerning the death of Mercer at Princeton.

> *for fuel to our guards, to keep up blazing fires until toward day, when they had orders to retire.*[40]

In a turn of good fortune for the Americans, a strong cold front swept into the area in the evening and froze much of the muddy, wet ground. Philemon Baldwin, one of the few Connecticut State Troops in Mercer's brigade that agreed to stay past his enlistment, described the impact of the cold front on the roads:

> *In the early part of the night* [of January 2nd] *the roads were muddy, the weather being moderate,* [but] *the weather suddenly became extremely cold* [and] *the surface of the earth was frozen & became hard as a pavement....*[41]

Major Wilkinson remembered that the darkness of the evening also favored the Americans:

> *The night, although cloudless, was exceedingly dark, and though calm and severely cold, the movement* [of the troops] *was so cautiously conducted as to elude the vigilance of the enemy.*[42]

General Washington provided Congress with his own account of the march preparations:

---

[40] Wilkinson, 140

[41] Selig, Harris, and Catts, *Battle of Princeton Mapping Project: Report of Military Terrain Analysis and Battle Narrative, Princeton, New Jersey,* Appendix I, Item 8, Pension Application of Philemon Baldwin

[42] Wilkinson, 140-141

> *I ordered all our Baggage to be removed silently to Burlington soon after dark, and at twelve OClock after renewing our fires & leaving Guards at the Bridge in Trenton and other passes on the…stream, marched by a roundabout Road to Princeton, where I knew* [the enemy] *could not have much force left and might have Stores.*[43]

Washington explained that he wanted to, *"avoid the appearance of a retreat,"* and hoped that, *"by a fortunate stroke* [at Princeton, he could remove] *Genl Howe from Trenton and give some reputation to our Arms…"*[44]

The American march commenced around midnight with General Mercer's brigade near the head of the column.[45] An unidentified American officer reported that, *"about five hundred men and two pieces of iron cannon were left* [behind] *to amuse the enemy."*[46] They had orders to abandon the lines before sunrise and disperse.

The fourteen mile night march to Princeton, like the one to Trenton a week earlier, was very difficult on the men. A soldier in Mercer's brigade recalled

---

[43] Chase and Grizzard, eds., "General Washington to John Hancock, 5 January, 1777," *The Papers of George Washington,* Vol. 7, 521

[44] Ibid.

[45] Stryker, 275

[46] An Account of the Battle of Princeton. From the Pennsylvania Evening Post, Jan. 16, 1777, "Extract of a Letter from an Officer of Distinction in General Washington's Army, Dated Pluckemin, Jan. 5, 1777," *Pennsylvania Magazine of History and Biography*, Vol. 8, No. 3, (Oct. 1884), 310

> *Our men were without shoes or other comfortable clothing; and as traces of our march towards Princeton, the ground was literally marked with the blood of the soldiers feet.*[47]

The half frozen and tired American troops marched through the night and halted in a patch of woods about two miles from Princeton just before dawn. While the troops briefly rested, General Washington organized the army into three divisions. The first and largest division (about half the army) fell under General Sullivan's command. Washington instructed Sullivan to, '*wheel to the right and flank the town,*" from the southeast, while the second division (composed of two brigades under General Mifflin) was to march left, destroy the bridge on the post road to Trenton that spanned Stony Brook, and approach Princeton from the northwest.[48]

General Mercer, with the third division (consisting of Mercer's and Stirling's combined brigade -- down to 350 troops and two cannon -- and General Cadwalader's 1,150 Pennsylvania militia and four cannon) was ordered to, "*march straight on to Princeton without turning to the right or left.*"[49] Mercer was eager to execute his instructions and trailed General Sullivan part of the way along the Saw Mill Road, leaving General Cadwalader's brigade, which was slow to resume its march, behind.[50] This created a large gap between Mercer and Cadwalader that would prove decisive.

---

[47] Sergeant R, "The Battle of Princeton," *The Pennsylvania Magazine of History and Biography,* Vol. 20, No. 1, 515

[48] Caesar A. Rodney, ed., *Diary of Captain Thomas Rodney, 1776-1777,* (Wilmington: Historical Society of Delaware, 1888), 33

[49] Ibid.

[50] Ibid., 34

Battle of Princeton

Just after sunrise, as General Mercer and his brigade passed Thomas Clark's farmhouse, they noticed the movement of troops on a hill less than a mile to the west (behind them and on their left).[51] General Washington, who was at the rear of Sullivan's division a quarter of a mile ahead of Mercer, noticed the troops as well. Major Apollos Morris, an aide-de-camp to Washington, witnessed his reaction and recalled that

> *Supposing this* [was] *a detachment sent out of Princetown to reconnoiter,* [Washington] *ordered Mercer's brigade, the next which followed, to quit the line of march, pursue and attack it.*[52]

Prior to the arrival of Washington's orders, General Mercer noticed a lone enemy horseman several hundred yards to the northwest who had approached the American column to investigate. A soldier in Mercer's brigade recalled that

> *About sunrise of the 3rd January 1777, reaching the summit of a hill near Princeton, we observed a light-horseman looking towards us, as we view an object when the sun shines directly in our faces. Gen. Mercer observing him, gave orders to the riflemen who were posted on the right to pick him off. Several*

---

[51] Selig, Harris, and Catts, *Battle of Princeton Mapping Project: Report of Military Terrain Analysis and Battle Narrative, Princeton, New Jersey,* Appendix I, Item 7, Undated "Memorandum of Gen. H. Mercer's ... services and character" by Lieutenant John Armstrong…

[52] Ibid., Appendix I, Item 90, Major [Apollos] Morris's Account of the Affair at Trenton, 1776

> *made ready, but at that instant he wheeled about, and was out of their reach.*[53]

The lucky horseman belonged to the same British detachment that General Mercer and Washington had noticed on the hill to the west. This detachment had marched out of Princeton an hour earlier to join Cornwallis at Trenton. Lieutenant Colonel Charles Mawhood, the commander of this British force, spotted part of General Sullivan's column at the same time that Washington noticed Mawhood, but from a mile away the British commander was unsure who the troops were, Hessians or rebels. Reports from his dragoons, including the one who had escaped Mercer's riflemen, convinced Mawhood that an American force of unknown size had slipped past him and threatened Princeton, so he immediately halted his march towards Trenton and redirected his detachment back towards Princeton.

Mawhood had with him two British regiments (the 17th and 55th Regiments of Foot) as well as an undetermined number of stragglers and convalescents from various regiments in Trenton who had become separated from their units but were now marching with Mawhood to rejoin them, plus approximately 50 cavalry and 50 dismounted cavalry from the 16th Light Dragoons and four cannon.[54] One other British regiment, the 40th Regiment of Foot, had remained in Princeton to guard the military stores left behind. They were

---

[53] Sergeant R, "The Battle of Princeton," *The Pennsylvania Magazine of History and Biography,* Vol. 20, No. 1, 516-517

[54] Selig, Harris, and Catts, *Battle of Princeton Mapping Project: Report of Military Terrain Analysis and Battle Narrative, Princeton, New Jersey,* 53

comfortably garrisoned at Nassau Hall (the College of New Jersey) oblivious to the approach of Washington's army.

As Lieutenant Colonel Mawhood marched back to Princeton with his troops, he learned of the presence of additional American columns trailing behind the one he initially spotted (Sullivan's). Mawhood concluded that he could not head off Sullivan's column, but he could attack the ones trailing behind (Mercer's), so he ordered the 55th Regiment (which was in the lead of his column) to continue on to Princeton to assist the 40th Regiment while he led the 17th Regiment and the rest of his detachment up a ridge to his right.[55] This brought them into William Clark's orchard and farm. Robert Lawrence, a local resident who lived near Clark, watched the British troops cross his land on their way to confront the rebels:

> *A Party of* [the British regulars] *came into our Field, and laid down their Packs there and formed at the corner of our Garden about 60 Yards from the door and then marcht away Immediately to the field of Battle Which was in William Clark's wheat field and Orchard Round about his house....*[56]

When the advance troops of Mawhood's force reached the crest of the ridge, they saw General Mercer's column marching straight towards them, unaware of the danger. The British troops deployed along a fence at the edge of William

---

[55] Ibid., 56

[56] Varnum Lansing Collins, ed., *A brief narrative of the Ravages of the British and Hessians at Princeton in 1776-77,* (Princeton: The University Press, 1906), 32-33

Clark's orchard and waited. A soldier in Mercer's brigade described what occurred when the two sides made contact:

> *We were descending a hill through an orchard,* [when] *a party of the enemy who were entrenched behind a bank and fence, rose and fired upon us. Their first shot passed over our heads cutting the limbs of the trees under which we were marching. At this moment we were ordered to wheel. As the platoon which I commanded was obeying the order, the corporal who stood at my left shoulder, received a ball and fell dead on the spot. He seemed to bend forward to receive the ball, which might otherwise have ended my life. They* [the British] *retreated eight rods* [about 40 yards] *to their packs, which were laid in a line. I advanced to the fence on the opposite side of the ditch which the enemy had just left, fell on one knee and loaded my musket with ball and buckshot. Our fire was most destructive; their ranks grew thin and the victory seemed nearly complete, when the British were reinforced.* [57]

Although Mercer's initial encounter with the British was victorious, the Americans soon found themselves outnumbered and in serious trouble. The remainder of Mawhood's detachment, along with several cannon, arrived on the scene and advanced towards Mercer's thin line spread along the fence.[58]

---

[57] Sergeant R, "The Battle of Princeton," *The Pennsylvania Magazine of History and Biography,* Vol. 20, No. 1, 517

[58] Ibid., and Selig, Harris, and Catts, *Battle of Princeton Mapping Project: Report of Military Terrain Analysis and Battle Narrative, Princeton, New Jersey,* 66

General Mercer's aide-de-camp, Lieutenant John Armstrong, claimed that the two sides clashed for fifteen minutes in the orchard, but other accounts describe a much shorter engagement, possibly only two or three volleys long.[59] British Captain William Hale, commanding a portion of the British stragglers and convalescents who were returning to their units in Trenton claimed that following a brief withdrawal of his troops from the fence he

> *Rallied* [his men] *with some difficulty, and brought them on with bayonets, the Rebels poured in a second fire...*[but] *the 17th Regiment advanced in a most excellent order, and at length we drove them through the railings, barns and orchards.*[60]

Another British account of the engagement asserted that

> *After two or three volleys, the column of the enemy began to give way; when the 17th regiment rushing forwards, with their bayonets drove the enemy back in their charge, on a line formed in their rear.*[61]

Many of Mercer's men lacked bayonets and could not stand against the British advance. One of Mercer's men remembered hearing General Mercer order a retreat in the face of it:

---

[59] Selig, Harris, and Catts, *Battle of Princeton Mapping Project: Report of Military Terrain Analysis and Battle Narrative, Princeton, New Jersey,* Appendix I, Item 7, Undated "Memorandum of Gen. H. Mercer's ... services and character" by Lieutenant John Armstrong...

[60] Ibid., Appendix II, Item 11, Letters written during the American War of Independence by the late Captain W. Hale , 45th Regt.

[61] Ibid., Appendix II, Item 2, *An Officer of the Army, The History of the Civil War in America*, Vol. 1

> *I soon heard Gen. Mercer command in a tone of distress, 'Retreat!'... I looked about for the main body of the* [American] *army which I could not discover –discharged my musket at part of the enemy, and ran for a piece of wood, at a little distance where I thought I might shelter.*[62]

General Mercer, whose horse had been struck in the leg by cannon shot, attempted to rally his men on foot, but the retreat had turned into a rout. Mercer passed back through the orchard with his men and was near William Clark's barn when a British soldier caught up to him and bashed him in the head with his musket butt.[63] He was then bayoneted several times by the British and left for dead.

Like most of the American army, Captain George Lewis, a nephew of General Washington from Fredericksburg who was well acquainted with General Mercer, believed several post-battle reports that the British had refused to accept Mercer's surrender and mercilessly bayoneted the stricken general while he lay on the ground.

General Washington even believed that his friend, General Mercer, had died on the field. When he learned (two days after the engagement) that Mercer had not died but in fact lay grievously wounded in a farmhouse in Princeton on parole, Washington sent Captain Lewis with Dr. Benjamin Rush under a flag of truce back to Princeton to tend to Mercer.

Upon joining Mercer at Thomas Clark's farmhouse (after he received permission from General Cornwallis) Captain

---

[62] Sergeant R, "The Battle of Princeton," *The Pennsylvania Magazine of History and Biography,* Vol. 20, No. 1, 517

[63] George Washington Parke Custis, *Recollections and Private Memoirs of Washington,* (Philadelphia: J.W. Bradley, 1861), 183-184

Lewis informed the wounded officer of, *"the extreme indignation which prevailed in the American army, together with threats of retaliation at the inhuman treatment it was supposed the general had received from the enemy, viz., that he had been bayoneted after having surrendered and asked for Quarter."*[64] General Mercer was greatly troubled by Lewis's comments and declared that

> *The tale which you have heard, George, is untrue. My death is owing to myself. I was on foot, endeavoring to rally my men, who had given way before the superior discipline of the enemy, when I was brought to the ground by a blow from a musket. At the same moment the enemy discovered my rank, exulted in their having taken the rebel general, as they termed me, and bid me ask for quarters. I felt that I deserved not so opprobrious an epithet, and determined to die, as I had lived, an honored soldier in a just and righteous cause; and without begging for my life or making reply, I lunged with my sword at the nearest man. They then bayoneted and left me.*[65]

General Mercer suffered several bayonet wounds, along with the blow to the head, and was left for dead on the field by the British.[66] He was not the only officer to fall from his brigade. Colonel John Haslet of Delaware, Captain Daniel Neil, the New Jersey militia commander of Mercer's two

---

[64] Ibid.

[65] Ibid., 184

[66] Selig, Harris, and Catts, *Battle of Princeton Mapping Project: Report of Military Terrain Analysis and Battle Narrative, Princeton, New Jersey,* Appendix I, Item 101, Letter of Dr. Potts to Owen Biddle, 5 January, 1777

cannon, (which fell into British hands) Captain John Fleming and Lieutenant Bartholomew Yates of the 1st Virginia Regiment were all killed in the brief, but heated, fight. The loss of these officers only added to the confusion and disorder of Mercer's troops; they fled rearward towards General Cadwalader's brigade, which had just arrived on the scene.

Cadwalader's 1,150 Pennsylvania militiamen easily outnumbered Mawhood's troops and advanced onto the battlefield to support Mercer's Brigade in a long column. General Cadwalader placed two cannon near Thomas Clark's house under Captain William Moulder and continued forward with his infantry.[67] Captain Thomas Rodney of Delaware was posted near Moulder's cannon and observed that

> *Gen. Cadwalader's Philadelphia Brigade came up and the enemy checked by their appearance took post behind a fence and a ditch in front of* [William Clark's farm buildings]; *on the hill behind the British line they had eight pieces of artillery which played incessantly with round and grape shot on our brigade, and the fire was extremely hot. Yet Gen. Cadwalader led up the head of the column with the greatest bravery to within 50 yards of the enemy, but this was rashly done, for he was obliged to recoil, and leaving one piece of his artillery, he fell back about 40 yards and endeavored to form the brigade, and some companies did form and gave a few volleys but the fire of the enemy was so hot, that, at the sight of the* [Mercer's] *troops running to the rear, the militia gave way and* [Cadwalader's] *whole brigade*

---

[67] Wilkinson, 143

> *broke and most of them retired to a woods about 150 yards in the rear.*[68]

For a brief time all that remained of American resistance to Mawhood was Captain Moulder's artillery, protected by a handful of intrepid infantrymen under Captain Thomas Rodney. Their determined stand near Thomas Clark's farmhouse stalled Mawhood's advance and allowed Cadwalader's and Mercer's brigades, bolstered by reinforcements from the rear of General Sullivan's column and rallied by General Washington himself, to reform and return to the battle. One of General Mercer's soldiers witnessed General Washington's efforts to rally the troops and remembered the commander-in-chief exclaim

> *Parade with us, my brave fellows, there is but a handful of the enemy, and we will have them directly.*[69]

The soldier noted that the effect of Washington's appeal was electric. "*I immediately joined the main body, and marched over the ground again.*"[70] Washington led the restored American line, strengthened by a portion of General Sullivan's division, forward. Mawhood's troops momentarily resisted, but they were significantly outnumbered and outflanked by the rebels and were forced to retreat. When a party of American riflemen moved around the British left flank to cut them off from Princeton, their retreat turned into a rout. The victorious Americans were urged on by General Washington who

---

[68] Rodney, ed., *Diary of Captain Thomas Rodney, 1776-1777*, 33
[69] Sergeant R, "The Battle of Princeton," *The Pennsylvania Magazine of History and Biography,* Vol. 20, No. 1, 517
[70] Ibid.

gleefully exclaimed, "*It's a fine fox chase, boys*!" [71] Some of Colonel Mawhood's men sought shelter in Nassau Hall, a large brick building in town. A blast of American artillery quickly convinced many to flee while the rest surrendered.

For the second time in ten days General Washington and his troops had surprised the enemy and routed them. At the cost of less than forty men killed and another forty wounded, the Americans inflicted a second stunning defeat on General Howe's army. British losses in killed, wounded, and captured numbered between 400 to 500 men.[72]

General Washington was tempted to continue eastward to attack the important British supply depot at Brunswick, but he decided against it because his men were exhausted and he knew that General Cornwallis was rapidly approaching from Trenton with 8,000 troops. Washington reluctantly directed his march north towards Morristown and the safety of New Jersey's mountains. He left behind scores of dead and wounded on both sides. A soldier from Mercer's brigade commented on the carnage:

> *"O, the barbarity of man! ... My old associates were scattered about groaning, dying and dead. One officer who was shot from his horse lay in a hollow place in the ground rolling and writhing in his blood, unconscious of anything around him. The ground was frozen and all the blood which was shed remained on the surface, which added to the horror of this scene of carnage.*[73]

---

[71] Ibid.
[72] Fischer, 414-415
[73] Sergeant R, "The Battle of Princeton," *The Pennsylvania Magazine of History and Biography,* Vol. 20, No. 1, 517-518

Battle of Princeton

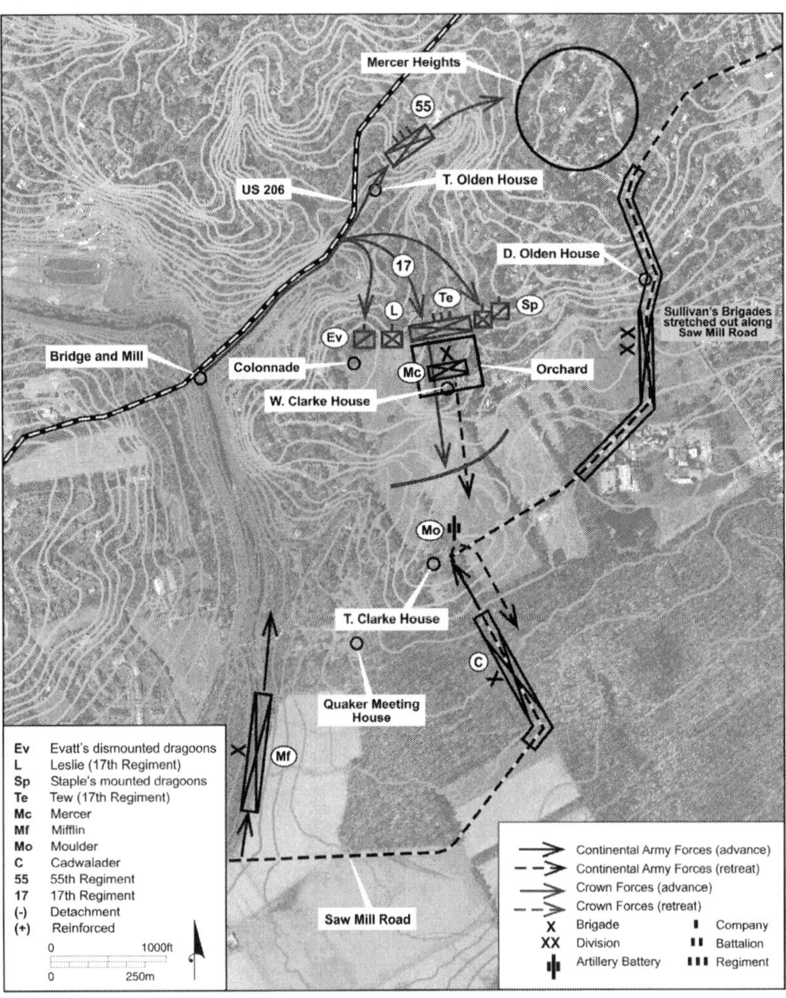

Figure 29. Movements of forces during the battle at Clarke's farm (Mawhood's Advance until American counterattack), 0830-0855.

Source: Battle of Princeton Mapping Project
Courtesy of Princeton Battlefield Society

Some of that blood belonged to General Washington's grievously wounded friend and brigade commander, General Hugh Mercer. Washington, aware that Mercer had fallen, was told in Princeton that Mercer's wounds were severe and mortal. There was nothing the commander-in-chief could do for General Mercer, and with General Cornwallis bearing down on Princeton, it was imperative that the victorious Americans escape and avoid a confrontation with Cornwallis, so General Washington departed Princeton under the assumption that General Mercer had died.

Death of General Mercer

General Mercer, who had lain on the frozen ground near William Clark's house while the battle raged about him, was in fact, still alive. He was discovered after the battle by his aide-de-camp Lieutenant Armstrong. Armstrong remembered that Mercer was, '*in a state of entire insensibility, the combined effect of the cold and his wounds*." Armstrong had his stricken commander taken to Thomas Clark's house for treatment.[74] Mercer apparently revived a bit on his way to the house for a soldier who claimed to help Lieutenant Armstrong carry Mercer recalled that although the general was, "*dangerously wounded…*[he] *exclaimed as he was carried along, 'Cheer up my boys, the day is ours'*."[75]

---

[74] William B. Reed, ed., *Life and Correspondence of Joseph Reed*, Vol. 1, (Philadelphia: Lindsey and Blakiston, 1847, 290

[75] Selig, Harris, and Catts, *Battle of Princeton Mapping Project: Report of Military Terrain Analysis and Battle Narrative, Princeton, New Jersey,* Appendix I, Item 56, Pension Application of Ensign John Hendy

Lieutenant Armstrong, assisted by Hannah and Sarah Clarke (sisters of Thomas Clarke who lived with him at the house that General Mercer was taken to) and Susanna, a recently freed female slave, tended to Mercer's wounds as best they could.[76] They were eventually joined by Dr. Jonathan Potts, whose examination of General Mercer was interrupted by the approach of General Cornwallis and his troops from Trenton.[77] Facing imminent capture, General Mercer ordered Lieutenant Armstrong and Dr. Potts to leave Clark's house and they reluctantly did so. Potts bitterly declared in a letter two days later that

> *I was obliged to fly before the Rascals, or fall into their hands.... Would you believe that the inhuman Monsters rob'd...General* [Mercer] *as he lay unable to resist on the Bed, even to the taking of his Cravat from his Neck, insulting him all the time.*[78]

Dr. Potts pessimistically added a grim prognosis for General Mercer's recovery in his letter:

> *General Mercer is dangerously ill indeed, I have scarce any hopes of him, the Villains have stab'd him in five different Places.*[79]

---

[76] L.B. Struble, "General Hugh Mercer," *Daughters of the American Revolution Magazine,* Vol. L, No. 4 (April 1917), 229

[77] Reed, ed., *Life and Correspondence of Joseph Reed,* Vol. 1, 291

[78] Selig, Harris, and Catts, *Battle of Princeton Mapping Project: Report of Military Terrain Analysis and Battle Narrative, Princeton, New Jersey,* Appendix I, Item 101, "Dr. Potts to Owen Biddle, 5 January, 1777

[79] Ibid.

Dr. Benjamin Rush, who arrived in Princeton on January 5th, to tend to General Mercer, was equally concerned about Mercer's condition, writing that

> *Mercer...received seven wounds in his body and two on his head, and was much bruised by the breech of a musket. His life was yesterday almost despaired of....*[80]

Mercer's condition appeared to improve overnight, however, and by the next morning Dr. Rush, announced that

> *I found* [General Mercer] *much relieved, and some of the most dangerous complaints removed, so that I still have hopes of his recovery, and of his being again restored to the arms of his grateful country.*[81]

General Washington was very relieved to learn that General Mercer was alive and sent a message to him through Colonel Joseph Reed:

> *When you see Genl Mercer be so good as to present my best wishes to him -- & congratulations (if the state of his health will admit of it) on his recovery from death. You may assure him, that nothing but the confident assertion to me that he was either dead – or within a few minutes of dying, and that he was put into as good a place as I could remove him to,*

---

[80] Dr. Benjamin Rush, *A Memorial Containing Travels Through Life of Sundry Incidents in the Life of Dr. Benjamin Rush,* 98

[81] Ibid.

prevented my seeing him after the Action, & pursuit at Princeton.[82]

General Cornwallis also offered his assistance in the care of General Mercer, sending his staff-surgeon to attend the gravely wounded general. Captain George Lewis was present when the British surgeon examined Mercer and recalled that

> *Upon an examination of the wounds, the British surgeon remarked, that although they were many and severe, he was disposed to believe that they would not prove dangerous.*[83]

Mercer's own medical knowledge and experience, however, convinced the wounded American commander that at least one of his wounds were fatal. Captain Lewis recalled that

> *Mercer, bred to the profession of an army-surgeon in Europe, said... "Raise my right arm, George, and this gentleman will then discover the smallest of my wounds, but which will prove the most fatal. Yes, sir, that is the fellow that will do my business."* [84]

Sadly, Mercer's prediction proved true, his wounds were fatal. Captain Lewis remained with Mercer until the end and recalled that

---

[82] Frank E. Grizzard Jr., ed., "General Washington to Joseph Reed, 15 January, 1777," *The Papers of George Washington,* Vol. 8, 76

[83] Custis, *Recollections and Private Memoirs of Washington,* 182-183

[84] Ibid.

> [Mercer] *languished until the 12th, and expired in the arms of Lewis, admired and lamented by the whole army. During the period that he languished on the couch of suffering, he exonerated his enemies from the foul accusation which they not only bore in 1777, but for half a century since, viz. of their having bayoneted a general officer after he had surrendered his sword and become a prisoner of war,-- declaring he only relinquished his sword when his arm had become powerless to wield it. He paid the homage of his whole heart to the person and character of the commander-in-chief, rejoiced with true soldierly pride in the triumphs of Trenton and Princeton, in both of which he had borne a conspicuous part, and offered up his fervent prayers for the final success of the cause of American Independence.*[85]

Reaction to Mercer's Death

General Mercer's body was taken to Philadelphia for burial where thousands turned out to pay their respects. On January 31st, Dixon and Hunter's Virginia Gazette published a letter from one who witnessed Mercer's funeral.

> *This day the body of the worthy and brave General MERCER was brought to this city, and interred with the military honors due to his rank and merit. In the death, or rather murder of the Gentleman, our country has lost a gallant officer and virtuous citizen.*[86]

---

[85] Ibid., 183-184

[86] Dixon and Hunter, *Virginia Gazette*, 31 January, 1777, 6

Purdie's gazette printed a similar letter that described General Mercer as, "*a soldier, a patriot, and a friend to the rights of mankind.*"[87] General Nathanael Greene undoubtedly agreed with this characterization of Mercer, confiding in his wife upon the news of Mercer's death that

> *He was a fine companion, a sincere friend, a true patriot and a brave General.*[88]

Congress wished to demonstration its admiration and respect for General Mercer and voted to erect a monument in General Mercer's honor in Virginia.[89] Congress also agreed to assume responsibility for the cost of General Mercer's newborn son's education. Similar arrangements were made for General Joseph Warren of Massachusetts (who died at Bunker Hill).[90] General Washington highly approved of these actions by Congress, writing soon after they were passed that

> *The Honors Congress have decreed to the memory of Generals Warren and Mercer, afford me the highest pleasure. Their character and merit had a just claim to every mark of respect, and I heartily wish, that Every Officer of the United States, emulating their virtues, may by their actions secure to themselves the same right to the grateful Tributes of their Country.*[91]

---

[87] Purdie, *Virginia Gazette*, 31 January, 1777, 2

[88] Richard Showman, ed., "General Greene to Catherine Greene, 20 January, 1777," *The Papers of General Nathanael Greene*, Vol. 2, (Chapel Hill, NC: University of North Carolina Press, 1980), 7

[89] Ford, ed., "8 April, 1777," *Journal of the Continental Congress*, Vol. 7 243

[90] Ibid.

[91] Philander, D. Chase, ed., "General Washington to Congress, 10 April, 1777," *The Papers of George Washington,* Vol. 9, (Charlottesville, VA: University of London Press, 1999), 112

Of all the tributes paid to General Mercer, however, the one offered by Major James Wilkinson many years later in his memoirs is probably the best:

> *In General Mercer we lost a chief, who for education, experience, talents, disposition, integrity and patriotism, was second to no man but the commander in chief, and was qualified to fill the highest trusts of the country.*[92]

Inscription on the Monument In Fredericksburg

Sacred to the Memory of HUGH MERCER, Brigadier-General of the Army of the United States:

He died on the 12th of January, 1777, of the Wounds He Received on the 3rd of the Same Month, near Princeton, in New Jersey, Bravely Defending the Liberties of America.

The Congress of the United States, in Testimony of his Virtues, and Their Gratitude, Have Caused This Monument to be Erected.

---

[92] Wilkinson, 147

Hugh Mercer Monument
Fredericksburg, Virginia

Appendix

Hugh Mercer's Last Will and Testament

March 20, 1776

In the name of God Amen. I Hugh Mercer of Fredericksburg in the county of Spotsylvania in Virginia Esquire do make this my last will and testament in an annex and form following that is to Say I desirest that after my decease my Dear wife Isabella, if she Survive me and my children on my plantation in King George County adjoining to Mr. James Hunter's land which plantation I Purchased from Gen. George Washington and that my executors Hereafter named out of my personal estate purchase or hire Negroes As they shall think best to work said plantation during my said Dear wife's lifetime for the benefit of her and all of my children equally,

but if she should object to the same then two ___ thereof for the benefit for all my children equally till my son William or the Child intitled thereto become of age and after her decease if she die before my said son William or child intitled come of age to work the whole until My said son or the child intitled become of age

and I do hereby order and desire my executors after named so repair the old house now Standing on that plantation or erect a new one for the ____ once of my said Wife and children aforesaid as they my said executors shall think Proper and pay the charges out of my personal estate

and after the Decease of my said Dear wife I give and devise one moity [share] of the said Plantation to my son William for his life and after his decease to the issue of his body lawfully to be begotten and the heirs & assigns to such issue remainder to my son John for life and after his decease...to issue remainder to such other child or children as I may leave at my decease or with which my said Dear wife may be ____ their heirs and assigns and as to the other moiety [half] of the said plantation I give the same to my son George for life and after his decease...with the remainder over to my other children and this as are ___ tted.

As for the fourth moiety In case my son William die without lawful issue I give & devise to my son William & his heirs two thousand acres of land on the river Kentucke in Fincastle County which I purchased of Mr. James Duncanson.

I give and devise to my son George and his heirs two thousand acres of land part of five Thousand acres surveyed for me by Warrant from the Govr. of Virginia in consequence of the Royal Proclamation of 1763.
I give and devise to my son John & his heirs three thousand Acres of land on the river Ohio about seventeen miles above the said river in the county of Fincastle which I purchased from Col. George Weedon,

I give and devise to my daughter Ann Gordon Mercer and her heirs one thousand acres of land on the river Ohio twelve miles above the falls of the said river in the county Fincastle which I purchased of Mr. James Duncanson Also one thousand acres of land on the river Ohio six miles above the Miami river which I purchased of the said Mr. Jas. Duncanson.

I give and devise to such child or children as my said Dr. wife is now [carrying] or may be born to me after my decease his /her or their heirs two thousand acres of land other part of the said five thousand acres surveyed for me by warrant from the Governor of Virginia as above mentioned.

I give to my executors hereafter Named & the survivors & survivors of them his or her heirs And assigns the houses & Lot which I bought of Mr. James Hunter adjoining to the Lot of Mr. Charles Dick whose only Family now resides also the Lot which I bought of Dr. John Sutherland Estate & the houses thereon adjoining the Lot of Mr. James Allen all situate in the town of Fredericksburg.

Aforesaid also the tract of land on the Fall Hill near Fredg. Aforesaid containing three hundred acres which I bought of Allen Wiley now in the [possession] of Reuben Zimmerman also three tracts of land on the river Yohogany near Stuart's Crossing called Mercerburg, Fredericksburg and Winchester containing nine Hundred acres, which I purchased from the proprietors of Pennsylvania upon the _____ ______ mentioned.

I also give to my said Executors and the survivors and survivors of them his or her Executors administrators and assigns my lease of a house in the Main in Fredericksburg aforesaid which I now hold from John Seldon on the same trusts with the Estates before given to them Viz upon trust to sell the same for the most & best price they can get for the same so soon after my decease as ___ shall be made and lands ____ their former Value otherwise at the end of ____ & to apply the money arising by such sale and the ___ & profits until such sale in general

I further direct my Books, D ___ Surgans Instruments, shop utensils & Furniture to be sold and also Such household furniture, Negroes or stocks of cattle and Horses as may ____ to my Executors hereafter names to be for the benefit of my personal estate & those intitled. Thereto the money assigns by such last mentioned sale ___ As to the rest of my personal estate all debts due from me by bond note of hand or open act are with all possible Expedition to be collected in as settled on bond with ___ Existing such debts as may be due from persons in indegent circumstances and as so two thirds of the Whole of my personal estate. I devise the same to Be equally divided amongst my children living at my decease and of which my said Dear wife may be _____ at my decease share and share alike the other third I direct to be Said and to the best advantage and the interest & _____ paid to my said Dear wife for her own use during her life and after her decease the principal divided amongst my children in the same manner as the former two thirds I give and devise all my real estate not herebefore disposed of equally amongst all my children born and to be born and their heirs equally provided always _______ and it is my express mind and will that if by any unforeseen accident the Grants & titles of my lands herebefore mentioned on the ohil, Kentucke, &

Yohogany Rivers should be ___annulled and rendered of no E___ then reserving to my said Dear wife her ____ of my real estate and the interest of one third of my personal estate for her life ___ my real estate to be all sold by my executors or the survivors or survivor of them his her or their heirs and assigns to whom I give the same for that purpose & the money arising thereupon together with my personal estate to be equally divided equally amongst all my children living at my decease or so be born afterward.

I do make constitute and appoint my Dear wife Isabella Mercer, Col. George Weedon, Doct. Jno Tennent of Port Royal and the daid James Duncanson Executors of this my will Hereby revoking all former wills by me made I declare this only to be my Last Will & Testament. Wrote on one side of two sheets of paper in witness Whereof I have to the first sheet set my hand and to This last sheet my hand and side this Twentieth Day of March in the year of our Lord one Thousand Seven Hundred and Seventy Six.

Witness by

John Francis Minor
John Bell
Elias Hardy

Executors were:

Isabella (his wife)

George Weedon

James Duncanson

Bibliography

Abbot, W.W., and Dorothy Twohig, eds. *The Papers of George Washington: Colonial Series,* Vol. 6-10. Charlottesville: University Press of Virginia, 1988-1995

Anderson, D. R. ed., "The Letters of Colonel William Woodford, Colonel Robert Howe, and General Charles Lee to Edmund Pendleton," *Richmond College Historical Papers*, June, 1915.

Anderson, Enoch. "Personal Recollections of Captain Enoch Anderson, an Officer of the Delaware Regiment in the Revolutionary War," *Papers of the Historical Society of Delaware,* Vol. 16. Wilmington: The Historical Society of Delaware, 1896.

Anderson, Fred. *Crucible of War*. New York: Vintage Books, 2000

Ballagh, James C., ed., *The Letters of Richard Henry Lee,* Vol. 1, NY: Macmillan Co., 1911.

Boatner III, Mark Mayo *Encyclopedia of the American Revolution.* NY: David McKay Co., 1966.

Boyd, Julian P. ed., *The Papers of Thomas Jefferson,* Vol. 1. Princeton, NJ: Princeton University Press, 1950.

Brock, R. A. ed., "Orderly Book of the Company of Captain George Stubblefield, 5th Virginia Regiment: From March 3, 1776 to July 10, 1776, Inclusive," *Virginia Historical Society Collections,* New Series 6, 1887.

Brock, R.A. ed., "Papers Military and Political, 1775-1778 of George Gilmer, M.D. of Pen Park, Albemarle Co., VA," *Miscellaneous Papers 1672-1865 Now First Printed from the Manuscripts in the Virginia Historical Society.* Richmond, VA, 1937.

Campbell, Charles, ed. *The Orderly Book of that Portion of the American Army Stationed at or near Williamsburg* 6th Regiment...*from March 18, 1776 to August 28, 1776.* Richmond, 1860.

Cecere, Michael. *They Behaved Like Soldiers: Captain John Chilton and the 3rd Virginia Regiment.* (Bowie, MD: Heritage Books, 2004.

Cecere, Michael. *Great Things Are Expected from the Virginians: Virginia in the American Revolution.* Westminster, MD: Heritage Books, 2008.

Chase, Philander D. ed., *The Papers of George Washington, Revolutionary War Series,* Vol. 1-9. Charlottesville, VA: University Press of Virginia, 1985.

Clark, William, ed., *Naval Documents of the American Revolution,* Vol. 1-2. Washington, D.C., 1964.

Collins, Varnum Lansing, ed., *A brief narrative of the Ravages of the British and Hessians at Princeton in 1776*-77. Princeton, NJ: The University Press, 1906.

Commager, Henry Steele. *Documents of American History.* New York: Appleton-Century-Crofts, 1963.

Cresswell, Nicholas, *The Journal of Nicholas Cresswell.* The Dial Press: NY, 1974.

Custis, George Washington Parke. *Recollections and Private Memoirs of Washington.* Philadelphia: J.W. Bradley, 1861.

Davies, K. G., ed. *Documents of the American Revolution,* Vol. 9. Irish University Press. 1975.

Drake, Francis, ed. *The Life and Correspondence of Henry Knox*. Boston, 1873

Dwyer, William M. *The Day is Ours! An Inside View of the Battles of Trenton and Princeton, November 1776 – January 1777*. New Brunswick, NJ: Rutgers University Press, 1998.

Felder, Paula S. *Fielding Lewis and the Washington Family: A Chronicle of 18th Century Fredericksburg*, The American History Company, 1998.

Felder, Paula S. *Forgotten Companions: The First Settlers of Spotsylvania County and Fredericksburgh Town.* Historic Publications of Fredericksburg, 1982.

Fischer, David Hackett. *Washington's Crossing* New York: Oxford University Press, 2004.

Force, Peter, ed., *American Archives*, Fourth Series, Vol. 4. Washington D.C.: U.S. Congress, 1848-1853.

Force, Peter, ed., *American Archives*, Fifth Series, Volume 1-3 Washington D.C.: U.S. Congress, 1837.

Ford, Worthington C. ed., *Journal of the Continental Congress,* 1774-1789, Vol. 4-5. Washington, D.C., 1906.

Goolrick, John T. *The Life of General Mercer.* New York: Neale Publishing Co. 1906.

Greenwood, Isaac J. ed., *The Revolutionary Services of John Greenwood… 1775-1783*. New York, 1922.

Hamilton, Stanislaus M., ed. *Letters to Washington & Accompanying Papers*, Vol. 5. Boston & New York: Houghton Mifflin, Co., 1902.

Hart, Sidney ed., *The Selected Papers of Charles Wilson Peale and his family, Volume 5, The Autobiography of Charles Wilson Peale.* New Haven and London: Yale University Press, 2000.

Hazard, Samuel ed. *Pennsylvania Archives*, Series 1,Vol.3. Philadelphia: Joseph Severns Co. 1853.

Henings, William W., *The Statutes at Large Being a Collection of all the Laws of Virginia,* Vols. 5-9. Richmond: J. & G. Cochran, 1821.

Hunt, Gaillard, ed., *The Writings of James Madison*, Vol. 1. New York: J.P. Putnam's Sons, 1900.

Jackson, Donald, ed. *The Diaries of George Washington.* Vol. 2-3. Charlottesville: University Press of Virginia, 1976.

Johnson, Henry P. *The Campaign of 1776 Around New York And Brooklyn: Including An Account of the Battle of Long Island and the Loss of New York*. Brooklyn, NY: Long Island Historical Society, 1878.

Kennedy, John Pendleton, ed. *Journals of the House of Burgesses of Virginia.* Vol. 10-13. Richmond, VA, 1905-07.

Ketchum, Richard M. *The Winter Soldiers: The Battles for Trenton and Princeton*. New York: Henry Holt and Co. 1973.

Lefkowitz, Arthur S. *The Long Retreat: The Calamitous American Defense of New Jersey, 1776*. Metuchen, NJ: Upland Press, 1998.

Loudon, Archibald, ed. *A Selection of Some of the most Interesting Narratives of Outrages Committed by the Indians in Their Wars with the White People,* Vol. 2. Carlisle, PA, 1811.

Marshall, John, *The Life of George Washington,* Vol. 2. Fredericksburg, VA: The Citizens Guild of Washington's Boyhood Home, 1926.

Mays, David John, ed., *The Letters and Papers of Edmund Pendleton,* Vol. 1. Charlottesville: University Press of Virginia, 1967.

Montgomery, Thomas Lynch, ed. *Pennsylvania Archives*, Series 5, Vol. 1. Harrisburg, PA: Harrisburg Publishing Company, 1906.

Montgomery, Thomas Lynch ed., *Report of the Commission to Locate The Site of the Frontier Forts of Pennsylvania*, Vol. 1. Harrisburg, PA: Wm. Stanly Ray, State Printer, 1916.

Parkman, Francis. *Montcalm and Wolfe: The French and Indian War*. New York: Barnes and Noble, 2005. Originally published in 1884

Reed, William B. ed., *Life and Correspondence of Joseph Reed*, Vol. 1. Philadelphia: Lindsey and Blakiston, 1847.

Reese, George ed., *The Official Papers of Francis Fauquier.* Vol. 2. Charlottesville: The University Press of Virginia, 1981.

Riley, Edward Miles, ed., *The Journal of John Harrower: An Indentured Servant in the Colony of Virginia, 1773-1776*, Williamsburg, VA: Colonial Williamsburg, Inc., 1963.

Rodney, Caesar A. ed., *Diary of Captain Thomas Rodney, 1776-1777.* Wilmington: Historical Society of Delaware, 1888.

Rowland, Kate Mason. *The Life and Correspondence of George Mason,* Vol. 1, New York: Russell & Russell, 1964.

Rush, Benjamin. *A Memorial Containing Travels Through Life or Sundry Incidents in the Life of Dr. Benjamin Rush.* Louis Alexander Biddle,1905.

Rutland, Robert, ed. *The Papers of George Mason.* Vol. 1. University of North Carolina Press, 1970.

Ryan, Dennis P. *Salute to Courage: The American Revolution as Seen Through Wartime Writings of Officers of the Continental Army and Navy.* NY: Columbia University Press,1979.

Schecter, Barnet. *The Battle of New York: The City at the Heart of the American Revolution.* New York: Walker & Company, 2002.

Scribner, Robert L., and Brent Tarter ed., (comps). *Revolutionary Virginia: The Road to Independence,* Vol. 1-7. Charlottesville: University Press of Virginia, 1973-1978.

Selby, John. *The Revolution in Virginia: 1775-1783.* Colonial Williamsburg Foundation, 1988.

Selig Robert, Matthew Harris, and Wade P. Catts. *Battle of Princeton Mapping Project: Report of Military Terrain Analysis and Battle Narrative, Princeton, New Jersey.* September, 2010.

Showman, Richard K. ed. *The Papers of General Nathanael Greene*, Vol. 1-2 Chapel Hill: University of North Carolina Press, 1976.

Smith, Paul H., ed., *Letters of Delegates to Congress: 1774-1789*, Vol. 1-4. Washington, D.C.: Library of Congress, 1976.

Stevens, S. K., Donald H. Kent, Autumn L. Leonard, eds. *The Papers of Henry Bouquet*, Vol. 2-5. Harrisburg: Pennsylvania Historical and Museum Commission, 1951.

Stryker, William S. *The Battles of Trenton and Princeton.* Old Barracks Association, 2001. Originally published in 1898

Ward, Harry M. *Duty, Honor or Country: General George Weedon and the American Revolution.* Philadelphia: American Philosophical Society, 1979.

Waterman, Joseph. *With Sword and Lancet: The Life of General Hugh Mercer*. Richmond, VA: Garrett and Massie, Inc., 1941.

James Wilkinson, *Memoirs of My Own Times*, Vol. 1. Philadelphia: Abraham Small, 1816.

Wrike, Peter Jennings, The Governor's Island: Gwynn's Island, Virginia During the Revolution, Gwynn, VA: Gwynn's Island Museum, 1993.

------- *The Lee Papers*, Vol. 1-2. Collections of the New York Historical Society, 1871.

------ Lieutenant Colonel Armstrong to Governor William Denny, 14 September, 1756," *Minutes of the Provincial Council of Pennsylvania,* Vol. 7. Harrisburg: Theo. Fenn & Co., 1851.

Periodicals

McMichael, James. "Diary of Lieutenant James McMichael of the Pennsylvania Line 1776-1778," *Pennsylvania Magazine of History and Biography,* Vol. 16, No. 2. 1892.

Peale, Charles Wilson. "Journal of Charles Wilson Peale, *Pennsylvania Magazine of History and Biography*, Vol. 38. Philadelphia: The Historical Society of Pennsylvania, 1914.

Powell, William S. ed. "A Connecticut Soldier Under Washington: Elisha Bostwick's Memoirs of the First Years of the Revolution," *The William and Mary Quarterly,* 3rd Series, Vol. 6, No. 1. Jan. 1949.

Reed, Joseph. "General Joseph Reed's Narrative of the Movements of the American Army in the Neighborhood of Trenton in the Winter of 1776-77," *Pennsylvania Magazine of History and Biography*, Vol. 8. 1884.

Sergeant R, "The Battle of Princeton," *Pennsylvania Magazine of History and Biography,* Vol. 20, No. 4. 1896.

Struble, L.B. "General Hugh Mercer," *Daughters of the American Revolution Magazine,* Vol. L, No. 4. April 1917.

Tyler, Lyon. "John Chilton to his brother, 30 November, 1776," *Tyler's Quarterly Historical and Genealogical Magazine,* Vol. 12. Richmond, VA: Richmond Press Inc., 1931.

------ An Account of the Battle of Princeton. From the Pennsylvania Evening Post, Jan. 16, 1777, "Extract of a Letter from an Officer of Distinction in General Washington's Army, Dated Pluckemin, Jan. 5, 1777," *Pennsylvania Magazine of History and Biography*, Vol. 8, No. 3, Oct. 1884.

Newspapers

New York Mercury, 4 October, 1756, 1

Pennsylvania Gazette, 3 May, 1759, 3

Purdie, *Virginia Gazette*, 6 June, 1771, 3

Purdie and Dixon, *Virginia Gazette*, "6 August, 1772," 2

Purdie and Dixon, *Virginia Gazette*, "9 July, 1772," 3

Purdie, *Virginia Gazette Supplement,* 5 May, 1775, 2

Purdie, *Virginia Gazette*, 9 February, 1776, 3

Purdie, *Virginia Gazette*, 1 March, 1776, 3

Purdie, *Virginia Gazette*, 5 April, 1776," 3

Purdie, *Virginia Gazette*, 19 April, 1776," 4

Dixon and Hunter, *Virginia Gazette*, 31 January, 1777, 6

Unpublished and Primary Sources

Dr. Hugh Mercer's Ledger Book 1771-73 on microfilm at the Simpson Library of the University of Mary Washington

Hugh Mercer's Will. *Spotsylvania County Records, Will Book E, 1772-1798.*

Selkirk, Malcolm G. *The Story of Hugh Mercer, Doctor, Soldier, and Jacobite,* Unpublished Manuscript, Perthshire, Scotland: 1991.

Index

C

D

E

H

I

J

K

L

M

N

O

P

Q

R

S

T

W

Y